Rats, Bulls, and Flying Machines

A History of the Renaissance and Reformation

by Deborah Mazzotta Prum

SERIES EDITOR John Holdren

WITH AN AFTERWORD BY E. D. Hirsch, Jr.

A CORE CHRONICLES BOOK

CONSULTING EDITORS:
Theodore Rabb, Princeton University
Duane Osheim, University of Virginia

ART EDITOR:
Tricia Emlet

DESIGN:
Bill Womack

ACKNOWLEDGMENTS:
This book has benefitted from the advice and suggestions of a number of readers, including not only our consulting editors, Professors Theodore Rabb of Princeton University and Duane Osheim of the University of Virginia, but also Byron Hollinshead, American Historical Publications; Dr. Mary Beth Klee (Founding Head of Crossroads Academy, a Core Knowledge school in Lyme, New Hampshire); Christiana Whittington (Music Teacher at Crossroads Academy); Tricia Emlet (Art Editor); and, at the Core Knowledge Foundation, Jeanne Siler, Michael Marshall, and Barbara Fortsch. Thanks also to fifth-grader Hannah Holdren for her helpful comments.

Library of Congress Catalog Card Number 99-072473

ISBN 1-890517-18-6 PAPERBACK
ISBN 1-890517-19-4 HARDCOVER

Core Knowledge Foundation
801 East High Street
Charlottesville, VA 22902
TELEPHONE: (804) 977-7550
FAX: (804) 977-0021
E-MAIL: coreknow@coreknowledge.org
HOME PAGE: www.coreknowledge.org

Printed in Canada

Dedicated to my grandparents:
Gaetano and Benedetta Boccaccio
Sebastiano and Santa Mazzotta

Contents

Part III The Reformation, *or Watch Out for the Papal Bull*

Europe in the Renaissance
about 1500

Check your library for a recent atlas so you can compare a map of Europe today to this map of Europe in Renaissance times. The boundaries of Spain, France, and Portugal in 1500 were close to what they are now. The Netherlands in 1500 has since become three countries. The biggest part of what was the Holy Roman Empire is now Germany. In Renaissance times Italy consisted of many independent city-states but is now one country. (See page 11 for a close-up map of the Italian city-states.) What other differences do you notice between Europe then and now?

Prologue
Rats and Bulls

Was it diseased rats that sparked the beginnings of the Renaissance? Or was it an Italian poet named Petrarch [PEH-trark] as he poked around in dusty old books?

What did a monk burning a papal bull have to do with the Reformation?

Just what *is* a papal bull, anyhow?

In this book, you'll read about rats and bulls (not the snorting kind), as well as artists, inventors, and a lot of other remarkable people who lived during the historical periods called the Renaissance and the Reformation.

Let's get started with the Renaissance. (Sorry, you'll have to wait till near the end of this book for that papal bull story.)

Part I The Renaissance in Italy: A Little History and a Lot of Artists

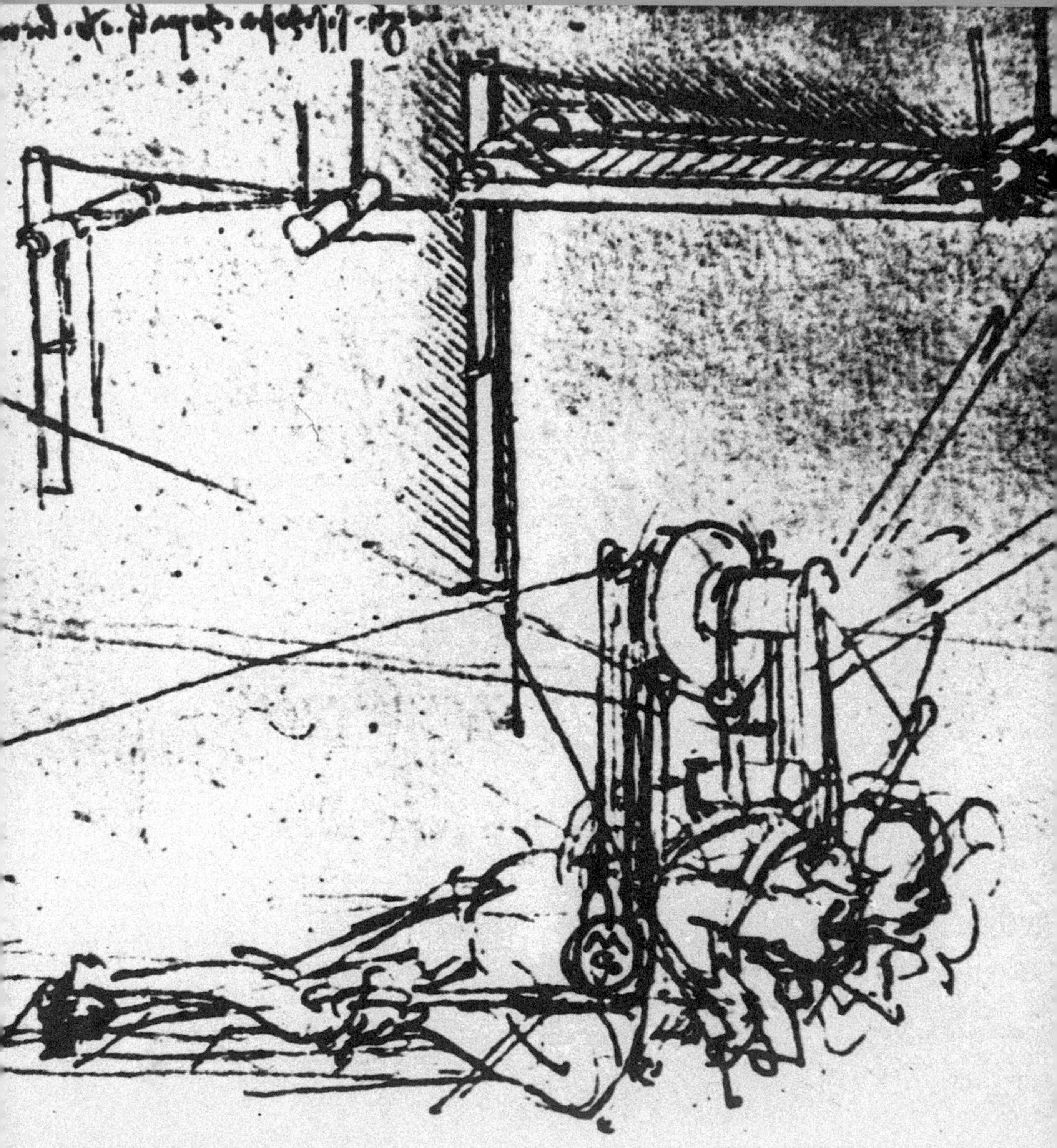

This is one of many ideas for flying machines that Leonardo da Vinci sketched in his notebooks.

Introduction
A True Renaissance Man

"I don't know why I let you talk me into this, Master Leonardo!" grumbled Carlo as he dragged an enormous contraption up the steep, rocky hill.

Leonardo da Vinci [duh VIN-chee] *laughed quietly and said, "Here, let me help." He steadied one huge wing of the flying machine as he walked alongside his servant.*

When they reached the summit, Leonardo gazed down at the streets and buildings of Florence. "Ah, Carlo, in a few moments, you will be sailing over our fair city."

"Master," sighed Carlo, "I wish it were you *who could experience that pleasure."*

Leonardo fastened the straps around his servant's thin shoulders and waist. "Done!" he cried as he tightened the last leather tie.

"Master," protested Carlo, "I look like a giant dragonfly!"

"Hush. If this works, your name will be known throughout history."

"If it doesn't work, I'll be *history!"*

Leonardo led Carlo to the edge of a high cliff. Carlo peered over, then made the sign of the cross.

"If you please, master," said Carlo, "has it occurred to you that if God had intended man to fly, He would have given us wings?"

But Leonardo just smiled and gave Carlo a hearty push off the cliff. As Carlo plummeted downward, Leonardo shouted, "Man can do anything he sets his mind to do, my faithless friend!"

I wish I could tell you that Carlo suddenly swooped upward and soared like a bird over the rooftops of the city of Florence. But, alas, the poor servant fell and broke his leg—or so goes the story that has come down to us over the years.

The story, whether true or legendary, tells a lot about Leonardo's attitude toward life. Those words were the theme of his career, and the theme of the Renaissance, too: Man is capable of doing anything he sets his mind to. Anything.

That belief drove Leonardo to explore uncharted territory in many fields. He was passionately interested in many subjects, and highly skilled at most anything he tried. Leonardo da Vinci was, in every sense of the term, a true Renaissance man.

Leonardo da Vinci is only one of the many extraordinary people you're going to meet in this book as you learn about the amazing times known as the Renaissance.

Let's begin with a little history.

You might hear people today refer to someone as a "Renaissance man." They mean someone who is well-rounded and skilled at many different things—for example, someone who is a scientist, painter, writer, and expert tennis player.

Chapter 1

Rats, Money, and Art: The Beginnings of the Renaissance

Happy Rebirthday

Renaissance—the word comes from a Latin word meaning "rebirth." The Renaissance was especially a rebirth of the arts and learning. It began in Italy, then spread through much of Europe. (See the map facing page 1.)

The Renaissance began around the year 1350 and lasted till the early 1600s. Historians don't agree on the exact dates, but they do agree on one point: the Renaissance was an exciting time of discovery and rediscovery. It was a time when new ideas were born and old ideas reborn.

What Came Before the Renaissance?

To understand why the Renaissance was such an amazing, extraordinary period, it helps to remember a bit about what was happening in Europe *before* the Renaissance. So, let's take a quick look back over a couple thousand years!

Historians call the thousand years before the Renaissance the *medieval* [me-dee-EEvul] era or the *Middle Ages*. They're called the Middle Ages because they happened in the middle of two great periods of art and learning. *After* the Middle Ages came the Renaissance, which you will be reading about in this book. *Before* the Middle Ages came the *classical* era, the time of the great civilizations of ancient Greece and Rome.

More than 2,000 years ago, from about 500 B.C. to A.D. 500, ancient Greece gave us extraordinary works of art like the Parthenon, as well as the ideas of great philosophers like Plato and Aristotle. Greece gave us lasting works of literature, including Homer's *Iliad* [ILL-ee-ud] and *Odyssey* [ODD-uh-see]. From Greece we have inherited important ideas about government, including the idea of democracy—rule by the people. (The

The ancient Greeks built the Parthenon as a temple to honor Athena, the goddess of wisdom.

Homer's *Iliad* and *Odyssey* and Virgil's *Aeneid* are called "epics." An epic is a long story that celebrates the feats of a great hero or heroes.

The ruins of the Colosseum, where chariot races and gladiator contests took place in ancient Rome.

Greek word *demos* means "people.")

Later, the ancient Romans built upon the ideas and achievements of the Greeks. The Romans also built great structures such as the Colosseum, and left us such powerful literature as the *Aeneid* [ih-NEE-id] by Virgil. The mighty Roman armies marched east and west and conquered a vast empire.

Historians generally say that the classical era ended and the Middle Ages began around the year A.D. 476, when the Roman Empire was invaded by fierce warriors who destroyed many cities and towns. For many years after the fall of Rome, people across Europe were cut off from each other. They lived in isolated towns and villages, with little trade or communication between them. For many people, life became a dreary routine of war, famine, and disease.

During the Middle Ages in Europe, the great writings of ancient Greece and Rome were almost forgotten, except here and there in the places called monasteries. Men who had devoted their lives to the Christian church, called monks, lived in the monasteries. (Women who devoted their lives to the church, called nuns, lived in similar places called convents.) The monks made beautiful copies of writings from ancient Greece and Rome. Back then there were no printing presses and, of course, no photocopiers. If you wanted to make another copy of a book, you had to do it by hand. While the monks helped keep knowledge alive, outside the monasteries life was often so hard that very few people had time to learn about science, math, philosophy, or art.

A monk at work

Most people in the Middle Ages had no time for learning.

Petrarch Says No to the Middle Ages

During the 1300s there lived a great Italian poet named Petrarch [PEH-trark]. He disliked the time in which he lived. He thought the Middle Ages were backward and dreary. He called them the "Dark Ages." Historians today don't agree with that term, but the name has stuck.

If Petrarch didn't like living in what he called the Dark Ages, what did he like? He preferred classical times, the times of ancient Greece and Rome. He saw them as a glorious time alive with learning. If you want to know the right way to live, said Petrarch, then look to ancient Greece and Rome. He filled his library with as many ancient books as he could find. He invited others to read and study these books as well.

Over the years, more and more of Petrarch's fellow Italians started to learn about the literature, art, and government of ancient Greece and Rome. They came to agree with

Petrarch. Ancient Greece and Rome were great civilizations, they said. Why, they asked, can't *we* be more like that?

These men who admired everything about ancient Greece and Rome were called *humanists*. They looked at life differently than the people of the Middle Ages. To understand how the views of the Renaissance humanists were new and different, first we need to look back to the way people thought in the Middle Ages.

A portrait of Petrarch

The Middle Ages are sometimes called "an age of faith." It was a time when the Christian religion was very powerful in Western Europe and the church was the most important part of the daily lives of many people. Everyone from rich noblemen to poor peasants gave money, materials, and sometimes their labor to help build the magnificent churches called Gothic cathedrals. These cathedrals, with their spires soaring toward the sky, seemed to point the way to heaven.

The spires on this Gothic cathedral in Cologne, Germany seem to point the way to heaven.

In the Middle Ages in Europe, people thought a lot about God and getting to heaven. They hoped for miracles to improve their dreary everyday lives. Their attention was focused less on this world than on the Christian promise of heaven—maybe because their lives were so hard that they needed the hope of a future paradise to help them get through the days.

In contrast, the Renaissance humanists were more interested in this world, in the here and now. While most Renaissance thinkers and artists were still religious people, they believed in the importance of what individuals could achieve in this world. An Italian architect, Leon Battista Alberti, summed up what you might call a Renaissance motto: "Men can do anything with themselves, if they will."

An architect is a person who designs buildings.

Why They Weren't the "Dark Ages"

You remember that Petrarch called the Middle Ages the "Dark Ages." If the name fit at all, it applied only to Western Europe, where invading tribes had conquered the once great Roman Empire. Elsewhere, however, the Middle Ages weren't dark at all. Instead they were years of great achievement in art and learning, especially in Byzantine

Calvin and Hobbes
by Bill Watterson
OK, YOU'VE ALL READ THE CHAPTER, SO LETS REVIEW.
CALVIN, WHERE WAS THE BYZANTINE EMPIRE ?
I'LL TAKE "OUTER PLANETS" FOR $100.
CALVIN AND HOBBES ©1993 Watterson. Reprinted with permission of UNIVERSAL PRESS SYNDICATE. All rights reserved.

[BIZ-un-teen] civilization and in Islamic civilization.

• *Byzantine Civilization:* When invading tribes destroyed and took over much of the Western Roman Empire, the Eastern Roman Empire remained strong. The Eastern Roman Empire is also known as the Byzantine Empire.

The great city of Constantinople was the center of Byzantine civilization. You can look at the map on page 8 to see Constantinople's location, which made the city an important link between Europe and Asia. From about A.D. 500 to 1200, Byzantine civilization was one of the most advanced in the world.

• *Islamic Civilization:* While it was hard for people in Western Europe to pursue learning during the Middle Ages, at this same time Islamic civilization was thriving. Many Muslim scholars were making big strides in math, science, and astronomy. Some scholars translated works by ancient Greek philosophers

This beautiful mosaic, made of small squares of colored glass, jewels, and precious metals, is located in a church in Ravenna, Italy. The figure wearing a crown is the empress Theodora, the wife of the emperor Justinian who ruled the Byzantine Empire from A.D. 527-65.

and scientists into Arabic, which helped preserve the classical writings. A great thinker and writer called Avicenna [ah-vih-SEN-uh] (his Arabic name was Ibn Sina), who lived around the year 1000, read many works by the Greek philosopher Aristotle, and went on to write his own works of philosophy, poetry, and astronomy. He also made important medical discoveries about how to treat diseases.

The religion of Islam was founded in Arabia in the seventh century by Mohammed. Followers of Islam are called Muslims. Muslims believe in one God; Muslims believe in the same God as Jews and Christians, although they call God by different names. The Arabic word for God is *Allah*. Islam spread quickly across Arabia, then into Africa and Europe. Today there are millions of Muslims all around the world.

Parts of Spain were conquered and settled by Muslims. Learning thrived in the Islamic cities of Cordoba, Granada, and Toledo. These cities were full of libraries, schools, and universities. In the tenth century, scholars from Africa, Asia, and Europe traveled to Cordoba to be part of a city so rich in the arts and learning.

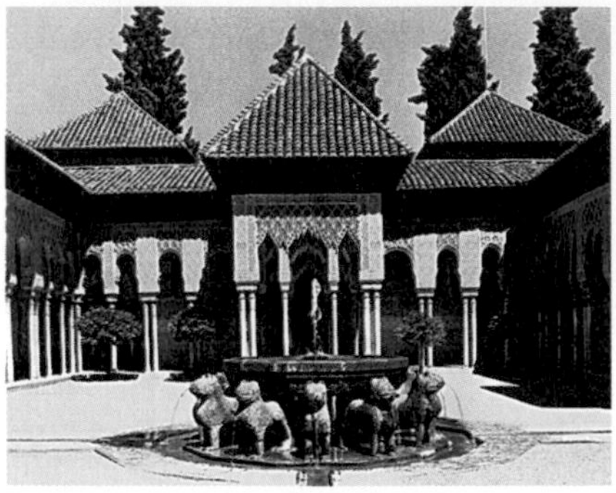

A beautiful example of Islamic architecture, this is the Court of the Lions, part of the Alhambra Palace in Granada, Spain.

Beginning in the late eleventh century, Christian forces started to drive the Muslims out of Spain. By the time of the reign of Ferdinand and Isabella—the king and queen who helped finance Columbus's voyage in 1492—the Muslims had been driven out of Spain. They left behind, however, writings about science and philosophy that would help spark the reawakening of learning in Italy during the Renaissance.

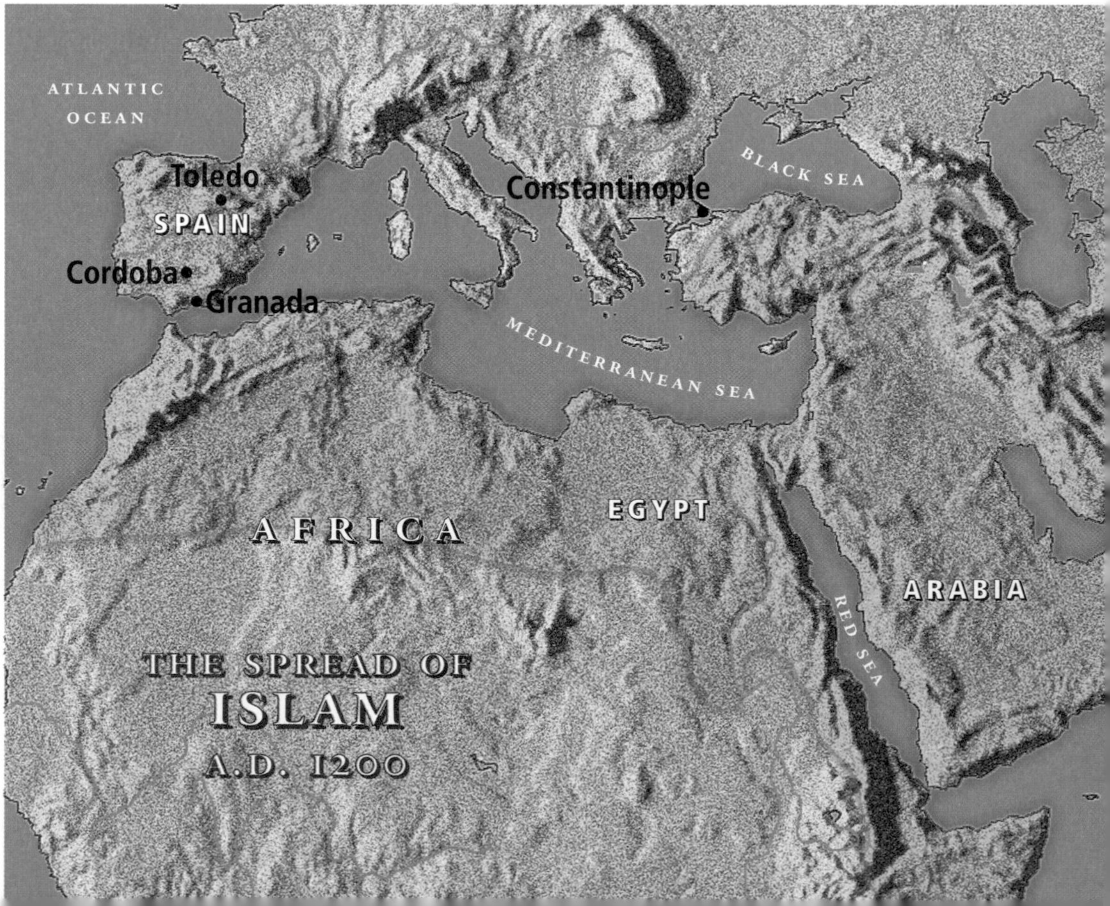

The religion of Islam began in Arabia in the seventh century A.D. then quickly spread far and wide. By the year 1200, Islam had spread farther east than this map shows, all the way to India, as well as west into Spain and North Africa.

extent of Islam

Rats Bring the Black Death

In the mid-1300s, trading ships sailed across the Black Sea and docked in Sicily, an island off the coast of Italy. Whatever cargo the boats carried for trade, they also brought something else—rats. The rats carried deadly diseases, including the bubonic plague. (A plague is a disease that spreads quickly among people.) Insects, especially fleas that sucked the rats' blood, carried diseases from rats to people. The bubonic plague gets its name from the lumps, called buboes, that swell up on people who catch the disease.

The Black Death killed millions.

This plague, called the Black Death, spread across Europe by the middle of the fourteenth century. It was called the Black Death because in the final stages of the disease, as a sick person had more trouble breathing, his skin would turn a dark purplish color. The plague was awful, devastating, terrifying. It killed *millions* of people, from one-third to one-half of the people living in Europe.

You know the nursery rhyme, "Ring around the rosie?" Did you know it comes from a rhyme about the Black Plague? The rhyme goes like this: **Ring-a-ring o' roses, / A pocket full of posies, A-tishoo! A-tishoo! / We all fall down.** The "roses" refer to a reddish rash that showed up on people with the plague. "A-tishoo" refers to another symptom of the disease, sneezing. "Posies" are herbs that people carried with them, hoping to keep away the disease—but the herbs were useless. "We all fall down" describes the sad end of the plague, when so many people fell down dead.

Italy: Location, Location, Location!

Something as terrible as the plague causes big changes in society. In Italy, the plague led to changes in business and trade, which turned out in the long run to be good for the country.

Here's how it happened. Because the plague killed so many people, there were fewer people to buy the grain and other products that Italian merchants were selling. Because there was more grain for fewer people, the merchants had to charge lower prices. But they were businessmen, and they wanted to make money. They knew they couldn't make money selling grain at such low prices. So they set out to find different products that they could sell at higher prices.

The Italian merchants started to sell wine, oil, cheese, and silk. Later, they began to sell leather items, fine furniture, and metalwork made by skilled craftsmen. Some businessmen figured out how they could make money by loaning other people money.

This Italian painting from 1470 shows a street scene with fabric and furniture merchants.

Italy became a great center of business and trade, not just because of the clever merchants, but for another big reason. If you've ever heard adults talk about starting a business or building a home, you might hear them say that there are three keys to success: "Location, location, location!" Italy was in the perfect location for business and trade. In the time of the Renaissance, many goods had to be transported by ship. Many of those ships sailed on the Mediterranean Sea.

Let's take a look at the map of Italy. But first you need to know this fact: even though we've been talking about Italy, back in the 1400s there was no single, unified country called Italy. Instead, what we now call Italy was made up of a bunch of powerful cities. The most powerful cities in the 1400s were Venice, Naples, Milan, Florence, and Rome. Each city, along with the region around it, made up a *city-state.* Each city-state was like a little, separate country. The city-states competed with each other to see who could have the greatest artists and the most splendid buildings. Sometimes they even fought against each other.

Even though Italy was not a single country at this time, we're going to call the whole region "Italy" because that's the name people recognize today. Now, look at the map on page 11. You can see that Italy is shaped like a boot and sticks out into the Mediterranean Sea. Port cities dot the coast. For example, find the important city called Venice. It is located in an ideal place for trade with Asia. Find the cities of Florence and Rome. Soon you'll read more about the great artists who worked in these cities. Now find the inland cities of Milan and Verona. They were well located for trade with countries in northern Europe.

All this trade meant more money. All this money caused more big changes in society.

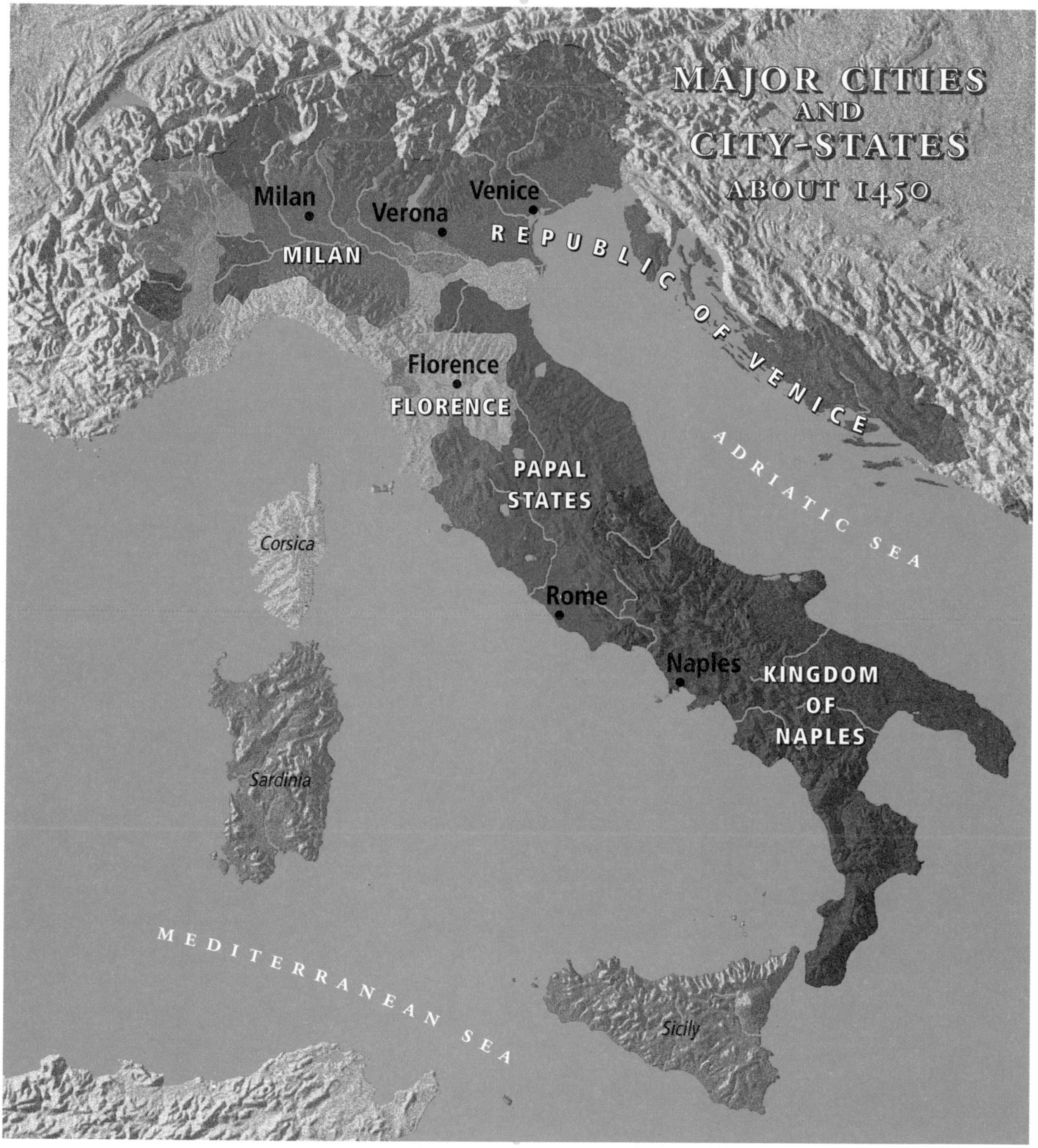

You've Got Class

Back in the Middle Ages, if you were born poor, you would probably stay poor. Society was roughly divided into three large groups, called classes, and whatever class you were born in, you pretty much stayed in. The three classes were:

- the nobility—wealthy people who ruled over large tracts of land
- the peasants—the people who worked for the noblemen
- the clergy—the people of the church.

From the late Middle Ages into the Renaissance, as the Italians became more wealthy and cities grew, there were more and more merchants and craftsmen—so many, in fact, that you could think of them as a new class. This was a *middle* class, between the peasants and the nobility. For the first time in recent history, you didn't have to be born a nobleman to be rich and powerful. You could work hard and make money and rise in society.

Craftsmen made up part of a new middle class.

Patrons: Dollars for Scholars

So what does all this about merchants and money have to do with the Renaissance? These wealthy businessmen could read and write. (Most people back then couldn't.) Some became interested in literature and art. Of course, most of them were so busy running their businesses that they didn't have time to write books or paint pictures themselves. But they had enough money to help others write, study, and make works of art.

Some of the merchants became *patrons* of the thinkers and artists. For example, a rich banker might ask an artist to paint portraits of his wife and children. The banker would pay for the portraits. In addition, he might provide the artist with food, clothing, and a house while he worked. With the support of such rich patrons, many artists were able to explore their ideas and develop their skills without having to worry about how they were going to eat or where they were going to sleep.

And what did the patrons get out of all this? What was their reward for paying artists to create paintings, statues, books, and buildings? It made them famous. The great patrons of the arts were admired and celebrated for the works they paid to have created.

So, How Did the Renaissance Come About?

There's no simple answer, but this much is for sure. Beginning in Italy in the mid-1300s, people rediscovered the culture and ideas of ancient Greece and Rome, which inspired them to think new ideas and attempt new artistic feats. Money from a new class of wealthy people—merchants, craftsmen, bankers, and more—helped those thinkers and artists follow their dreams.

Now it's time to meet one of the richest and most powerful families of Renaissance Italy.

Chapter2

The Medici of Florence, the Pope in Rome, and the Merchants of Venice

By the mid 1400s, Cosimo [KOZ-ih-moe] de' Medici had built a thriving international banking business. He and his family made the city of Florence the banking center not just of Italy but of all of Europe.

Like his ancestors, Cosimo was a shrewd businessman. He knew how to make a lot of money. Something else also captured his interest.

Cosimo had grown up surrounded by the ruins of the Roman Empire. As a child, he had looked at the crumbling buildings and wondered: Who were these Romans? What did they think? What can I learn from them?

Legend has it that as a young boy, Cosimo approached his father, Giovanni de' Medici, and begged a favor. You can imagine a conversation something like this:

"Papa, please give me some money so that I may go to Jerusalem."

Giovanni stared at his son. (In those days, getting to Jerusalem would be about as difficult and expensive as it would be for you to get to the North Pole.) "Jerusalem?" he asked. "Why, my boy? Do you want to make a religious pilgrimage?"

A pilgrimage is a religious journey to a sacred place.

A view of Florence

A Banker Who Loved Art

Medici [MED-ih-chee]—when you hear the name of this rich and powerful Renaissance family, think of two things: art and money.

The Medici family lived in the city of Florence. In the early 1300s, the Medicis were one of the Italian families who figured out the basic principles of banking. They got rich by making money work for them. (See the box on page 15.)

"No. But I've heard that's where I can find wonderful old books written by the ancient Greeks and Romans. Father, I want to find those books!"

Giovanni said no. (If you asked for money and permission to go to the North Pole, do you think the answer would be yes?) His father's refusal didn't discourage young Cosimo. From then on, he wanted to learn about classical art, literature and philosophy.

Remember, "classical" means anything pertaining to the ancient Greeks and Romans, including their art, literature, and philosophy.

When he grew up, Cosimo collected rare books and manuscripts. He hired scribes to recopy and translate them. He built libraries to hold the books. He invited scholars to read and study them. He made sure that his own children read great works by the Roman poet Virgil and the Greek philosopher Plato.

A manuscript is a book or other document written out by hand. The word comes from two Latin words, *manus* (hand) and *scriptus* (written).

Truth and Beauty

Cosimo was a great patron of the arts. The Medici house became a gathering place for thinkers and artists from around the world. Many artists lived with Cosimo as they worked on their statues and paintings.

In 1453, the great city of Constantinople was conquered by the Ottoman Turks, who changed the name of the city to Istanbul, as it's called today. (See the map on page 8.) When the Turks attacked, many scholars fled from Constantinople to Italy. They brought with them works of art and precious books preserved from the days of ancient Greece and Rome. Many Italians, including Cosimo de' Medici, welcomed these men, their books, and their ideas.

Architects, philosophers, sculptors, and merchants shared meals and lively conversation in Cosimo's home. They admired the Greek philosopher Plato and formed a club they called the Platonic Academy. These men believed, as Plato did, that the study of beauty would help a person understand what is true.

Cosimo collected art like this statue of the Greek goddess Hera.

Cosimo and many of these men collected coins, medals, and pieces of statues from ancient times. The art Cosimo owned made him famous. His impressive collection made people feel even greater respect for his power and authority.

Who's Really in Charge?

One idea from the ancient Greeks really appealed to Cosimo. This was the idea of democracy—rule by the people. Cosimo liked the idea of creating a new society in Florence modeled on Greek ideas. But for Cosimo, democracy was only an idea. In reality, the city of Florence was not run in a democratic way. In reality, Cosimo controlled Florence.

Here is the way democracy was supposed to work in Florence. The craftsmen and merchants of Florence joined together in special groups called *guilds*, such as the wool merchants' guild, the silk weavers' guild, and the doctors' and pharmacists' guild. The guild members elected councilmen, and these councilmen were supposed to govern the city.

That was a step toward democracy. But it was Cosimo who told guild members which councilmen to elect. These men were friends of his who followed his suggestions closely. By this method, Cosimo ruled Florence for thirty years.

The citizens of Florence liked Cosimo well enough that they did not protest his way of ruling the city. After all, Cosimo successfully protected the city from its enemies. He made generous gifts to charity. Business in Florence was booming.

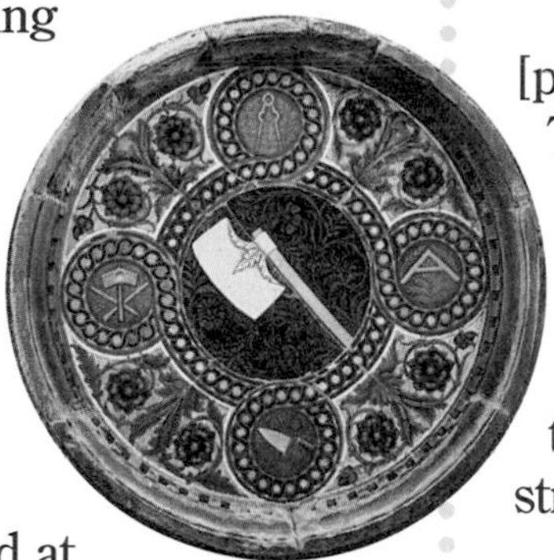

The coat of arms of the Carpenters and Builders Guild of Florence

When Cosimo died at the age of seventy-six, the grateful people of Florence gave him the title "Father of Our Country."

How Bankers Made Money, *or* That's Interesting

1. Money-changing: Renaissance bankers would charge a fee to exchange foreign money for local money. For example, they would take francs (French money) and exchange them for florins (Italian money). Then they would charge a few extra florins for the service.

A Renaissance banker and his wife

2. Loaning Money: The bank would loan money to a customer. The customer would promise to pay back the money, plus an added charge called *interest*. For example, if you borrowed $100 and promised to pay 10 per cent interest, you would have to repay the bank $110.

3. Bills of Exchange: A bill of exchange was like a modern-day traveler's check. During the Renaissance, robbers often attacked traveling merchants. So instead of carrying cash with them, some merchants brought papers issued by a bank. These bills of exchange allowed them to take out money from a bank in another country. They weren't much good to a robber who wanted cash.

Like Father, Not Like Son

After Cosimo's death, his son Piero [pee-AIR-oh] took charge of Florence. The people gave him a title too, but it was not as glorious as his father's. They called him "Piero the Gouty," because he suffered from gout, a painful disease of the joints. He had to be carried from place to place on a stretcher.

Piero did not inherit his father's leadership or banking skills, though he did inherit his father's love of the arts. Piero filled the Medici home with works of art from all over the world. But frail Piero ruled only a few years before he died. Piero's son, Lorenzo, became ruler of Florence when he was only twenty years old.

Lively, dashing, and popular, Lorenzo was the opposite of his sickly father. He played sports, wrote songs, and loved to discuss poetry and philosophy. Lorenzo enjoyed the good life so much that when his father died, he hesitated to take charge of Florence. He soon realized, however, that in Florence, if you weren't in charge, you wouldn't stay wealthy.

Murder in the Cathedral

Right after Lorenzo took control of Florence, he faced a serious threat to his rule. One day, he and his younger brother Giuliano were worshiping in church. Suddenly, men from a rival banking family burst through the doors and attacked them.

The men murdered poor Giuliano on the spot. Lorenzo was badly wounded but he managed to escape. Other people in the church chased down the assassins and hanged them.

A bust of Lorenzo de' Medici

Over the next few months, Lorenzo took charge. He made peace with some of his enemies, but he gave orders for others to be killed. To his credit, he managed to keep Florence from getting into what could have been a bloody war. His peacemaking skills won the hearts of his countrymen and the respect of other leaders in Europe. People began to call him "Lorenzo the Magnificent."

Patron and Poet

Like his father and grandfather, Lorenzo loved classical literature and art. He wrote poetry. The Platonic Academy continued to meet at his house. He carried on the family tradition of supporting many painters and sculptors and filling his home with beautiful works of art.

Lorenzo started the school of sculpture where the great Michelangelo trained as a young boy. Some stories report that Michelangelo carved animals in the snow to entertain Lorenzo's children. (Michelangelo would go on to carve some of the greatest statues in the world. You'll read more about him in this book.)

Severe Savonarola

Lorenzo had ruled Florence for about ten years when a preacher named Savonarola [sah-vo-nah-ROW-la] came to the city. Little did Lorenzo know the trouble this preacher would bring. As soon as Savonarola arrived in town, he began preaching against the Medicis. He said they ate too much, drank too much, dressed immodestly, and cared too much about their fancy belongings. He made the same charges against the people of Florence.

Lorenzo tried to make peace with Savonarola by giving a donation to the monastery where the monk lived. Savonarola returned the money with an insult. He said a good monk is "like a good watchdog—when a thief comes along and throws him a bone, he puts it to one side and goes on barking."

Savonarola

The End of the Medicis, and Goodbye Savonarola

In 1492, Lorenzo died at the age of forty-three, leaving his twenty-one year old son Piero in charge. This Piero was known as "Piero the Unlucky" and "Piero the Foolish," which gives you a pretty good idea of how well he governed Florence.

Two years later, the French invaded Florence, and Piero was forced to leave the city. Angry mobs broke into the Medici home and tore it to pieces, destroying and selling off many valuable items.

After Piero's departure, Savonarola took charge of the city for a while. He had a grand plan to turn Florence into a model city of Christian virtue. But his expectations were too high, and his rules were too strict. For example, he sent out bands of men who patrolled the streets and carried sticks to beat anyone whose clothing they thought was too fancy.

Although Savonarola's message was harsh, many people listened to him. Once he urged his followers to build a huge bonfire in the town square. He told the people of Florence to throw in their "vanities," the things he considered

I wouldn't wear that if I were you.

fancy and unnecessary. Men and women tossed jewelry and expensive clothing, even paintings and books, into the roaring blaze, which is remembered as the "bonfire of the vanities."

Although Savonarola was a monk, he loudly insulted the powerful leader of the church, the pope. He said that Pope Alexander VI was corrupt. Savonarola didn't mince words—he said, among other things, that the pope worked for Satan!

At first, the pope ordered Savonarola to stop giving sermons. This didn't quiet the angry monk. Later, the pope excommunicated Savonarola, which means he took away his membership in the church. Then Savonarola was accused of the crime of heresy—of holding beliefs that disagreed with the church. Back then, the church was very powerful and demanded that people follow its rules. It was a serious crime to be a heretic—so serious that when Savonarola was found guilty, he was hanged, then his body was burned in the town square.

From Florence to Rome

The main activity of the Renaissance now moved from Florence to Rome. Rome was the headquarters of the Catholic church. And the pope, as you know, was the head of the church. From about 1450 on, one pope after another took on the role of patron of the arts. Like the wealthy businessmen of Florence, the popes in Rome decided to support artists in their work.

Why? Pope Nicholas V said that when people saw majestic buildings, gorgeous paintings, and beautiful sculpture, they would think about the glory of God and their faith would be strengthened. Also, the popes thought people would better appreciate the magnificence and power of the church when they saw the spectacular works of art created with the church's support.

The popes called many artists to Rome and set them to work on some of the most beautiful paintings, sculptures, and buildings of all time. Rome replaced Florence as the cultural center of the Renaissance.

The Vatican and St. Peter's

The pope lives in the Vatican, a short name used for the Palace of the Vatican. This huge building contains the official home of the pope, as well as many museums, chapels, church offices, and a library. It is located in what is now called Vatican City. Vatican City used to be a part of Rome, but now it's a separate country. (That's right, Vatican City is now a country—in fact, it's the smallest independent country in the world.)

St. Peter's Basilica

One of the most important buildings in Vatican City is St. Peter's Basilica, which was designed and built mostly during the Renaissance. St. Peter's is a great church that was looked upon as something like the capitol of Christianity.

Julius II: Warrior and Patron

No pope was more determined to restore the power and glory of the Catholic church than Julius II. In shining armor, riding his powerful war horse, he himself led his armies into battle to get back the land around Rome that earlier popes had lost. He drove back the French from the northern frontier of Italy.

Pope Julius II

Julius pushed his men hard and accepted no excuses. Once, his soldiers and their horses were stuck in chest-high snow. When Julius heard that the army was unable to move forward in the deep snow, he came out and beat the soldiers and their horses with his cane.

Pope Julius II was more than a warrior. He was also the greatest patron of the arts among the Renaissance popes. He wanted to restore the glory of the church by acquiring great works of art and paying for magnificent new buildings. You'll read more about this soon when we look at the life and works of Michelangelo, one of the great artists whom Julius supported.

Venice: The Floating City

From Florence and Rome, two of the great Renaissance city-states, let's move northward to Venice. The Republic of Venice was the great trading center of the Renaissance. Look at the map on page 11 and you'll see why. The city of Venice is perched on the Adriatic Sea, between Europe and Asia. Even in the Middle Ages, the merchants of Venice were trading in Constantinople and as far away as China. The Venetians [vuh-NEE-shuns], as the people of Venice are called, loaded their ships with silver, wine, and woolen cloth from Europe, as well as fine glassware produced right in Venice, to trade with merchants to the east. They returned with silk and porcelain from China or

Gondolas float on the Grand Canal in this 15th century painting by Vittore Carpaccio.

spices from the East Indies. Ships from Venice also carried many thousands of people on pilgrimages to the city of Jerusalem in the Holy Land.

By the fifteenth century, Venice had built a fleet of ships and won battles to take over neighboring city-states. Venice became so wealthy and powerful that the city was called "the Queen of the Adriatic."

Venice is a city on the water—not just near but *on* the water. The city isn't built on a solid mass of land but rests on more than a hundred small islands. To connect many of the islands, the Venetians built bridges as well as a maze of narrow waterways. These waterways, called canals, crisscrossed the city and made it possible to get from one little island to another. The most famous of the canals, the Grand

In the year 1271, Venice's most famous traveler, seventeen-year-old Marco Polo, set off with his father and uncle on a four-year journey across deserts and mountains that took them finally to China. They arrived at a palace of marble and gold, the home of Khubilai Khan, the ruler of China. Many years later back in Venice, Marco Polo was taken prisoner during a sea battle. In prison, Marco told stories of all the wealth and wonders he had seen, while a fellow prisoner wrote down what Marco said. Soon after Marco was released from prison in 1299, *The Travels of Marco Polo* was published, and it opened the eyes of Europeans to lands and people in Asia that they knew nothing of before. The book remained popular into the Renaissance. One reader of the book was so fascinated that he decided to travel to the lands Marco Polo had visited. But when Christopher Columbus set sail in 1492, he didn't reach Asia because—well, you know what happened.

This painting done by Gentile Bellini in about 1500 shows a religious ceremony taking place in St. Mark's Square, with St. Mark's Basilica in the background. Like many buildings in Venice, the Basilica's architecture combines classical style with Byzantine influences, such as the domes you can see here.

Canal, winds through the city for about two miles. In Renaissance times, people traveled on the canals in long, sleek, flat-bottomed boats called gondolas. (Even today, gondolas carry many tourists on the canals of Venice, but now they share the waters with motorboats.)

During the Renaissance wealthy Venetians not only supported many artists, they also built a city that is a work of art. At the heart of the city's life is the huge open area called St. Mark's Square, where thousands of pigeons flock before the doors of the magnificent church called St. Mark's Basilica. In 1495, a French ambassador wrote that Venice "is the most triumphant city I have ever seen, the most respectful to all ambassadors and strangers, governed with the greatest wisdom, and serving God with the most solemnity."

Chapter3

Someday My Prince Will Come: Power in the Renaissance

Do the Ends Justify the Means?

Have you ever heard someone say, "The ends justify the means?" When someone uses that expression, he or she is saying that as long as you achieve your goals—your "ends"—it's okay to use any methods—any "means"—to do so.

A lot of people think that the expression "the ends justify the means" came from a man who lived in Florence during the Renaissance, Niccolò Machiavelli [MAHK-ee-uh-VEL-lee]. Actually, Machiavelli never said those exact words. But let's see why so many people associate him with "the ends justify the means."

Remember how during the Renaissance there was a rebirth of interest in ancient Greece and Rome? Machiavelli certainly felt such interest. In a letter he wrote to a friend, Machiavelli said that he wrote *The Prince* after reading many works of history by "the ancients," the classical writers of Greece and Rome. "I give myself completely over to the ancients," Machiavelli said. While reading them, he said, "I feel no boredom and forget every worry."

Machiavelli and *The Prince*

Niccolò Machiavelli entered the scene in Florence after the Medicis lost power and Savonarola died. He worked in the government of Florence for many years. During that time, he saw all sorts of fighting. He saw vicious struggles between the city-states in Italy, between city-states and foreign countries, and between the pope and other rulers.

Niccolò Machiavelli

All this fighting among rulers made him think. He thought about how a prince should rule his people. Because of all the fighting, he especially thought about how a prince should defend himself against enemies and remain in power. He wrote his ideas in a famous book called *The Prince.*

What is the chief goal of a prince? To stay in power, said Machiavelli. Machiavelli even said that to keep his power, a prince might have to lie, cheat, and steal. "A wise leader," Machiavelli wrote, "cannot and should not keep his word when keeping it is not to his advantage."

Machiavelli asked, "Is it better [for a prince] to be loved than to be feared, or the reverse?" What do you think? If you were a powerful ruler, would you want your people to love you or fear you?

Machiavelli said that a prince should wish to be both loved and feared. But he also said that if a ruler had to choose one or the other, then it would be better for people to fear him. Why? Because people who are scared of you are easier to control.

These ideas and others have given Machiavelli a bad reputation over the years. Even today, if you describe someone as "Machiavellian," you mean that person is crafty, sneaky, power-hungry, and willing to use any means to achieve his ends.

FROM *THE PRINCE*

•

"ANYONE WHO DETERMINES TO ACT IN ALL CIRCUMSTANCES THE PART OF A GOOD MAN MUST COME TO RUIN AMONG SO MANY WHO ARE NOT GOOD. HENCE, IF A PRINCE WISHES TO MAINTAIN HIMSELF, HE MUST LEARN HOW NOT TO BE GOOD, AND TO USE THAT ABILITY OR NOT AS IS REQUIRED."

•

"THE EXPERIENCE OF OUR TIMES SHOWS THAT THE PRINCES WHO HAVE DONE GREAT THINGS ARE THE ONES WHO HAVE TAKEN LITTLE ACCOUNT OF THEIR PROMISES AND WHO HAVE KNOWN HOW TO ADDLE THE BRAINS OF MEN WITH THEIR CRAFT."

•

"IF MEN WERE ALL GOOD, THIS ADVICE WOULD NOT BE GOOD, BUT SINCE MEN ARE WICKED AND DO NOT KEEP THEIR PROMISES TO YOU, YOU LIKEWISE DO NOT HAVE TO KEEP YOUR PROMISES TO THEM."

•

"SO FAR AS HE IS ABLE, A PRINCE SHOULD STICK TO THE PATH OF GOOD BUT, IF THE NECESSITY ARISES, HE SHOULD KNOW HOW TO FOLLOW EVIL."

•

Get Real!

Some historians think Machiavelli doesn't deserve his bad reputation. They say he was a wise man who preferred a government in which the people had a say, as it had been back in the Roman Republic. They say that in *The Prince* Machiavelli was just being realistic. He was simply describing what men really do, not what they *say* they do.

But others disagree. They think that Machiavelli had too dark and pessimistic a view of human nature. They think that people aren't as bad as Machiavelli thought. Look above at the quotations from *The Prince*. Read them and see what you think.

The Bad Borgias

When Machiavelli wrote about princes who didn't keep their promises, he often had in mind the Borgia [BOR-juh] family.

Most historians agree that the Borgias were cruel, dangerous, and violent people. Rodrigo Borgia, who became Pope Alexander VI, holds the unpleasant reputation of being one of the most corrupt popes of all times. (Remember, Savonarola said he worked for Satan!) In *The Prince*, Machiavelli wrote this about Alexander VI: "There never was a man more effective in swearing that things were true, and the greater the oaths with which he made a promise, the less he observed it."

Cesare Borgia

Rodrigo Borgia had a son named Cesare [CHAY-zah-ray]. Cesare Borgia was a brute. His father put him in charge of an army. Machiavelli traveled with Cesare at times and was impressed by his military skills. Cesare knew how to get power and keep it. He ruthlessly tried to conquer everything that lay in his path.

When Cesare decided he wanted to take possession of the city of Camerino, he visited his friend, the Duke of Urbino. Cesare asked to borrow all the cannons of Urbino so he could use them to attack Camerino.

The Duke, a trusting man, agreed to Cesare's request. But that night, Cesare marched back into his friend's city and conquered Urbino with its own cannons!

Later, Cesare went on to capture Camerino by deception, too. He negotiated with the rulers of the city. If they would surrender, then Cesare promised to let them off easy. They agreed to surrender. Then Cesare betrayed them. As soon as Cesare and his army entered the city, he gave orders for the rulers to be strangled.

Fortunately, the Borgias did not stay in power long. Pope Alexander VI died in 1503. Some say he had malaria. Some say he was poisoned. No doubt a lot of people wanted to poison him!

When his father died, Cesare was chased out of Italy. He died in battle in Spain at the age of thirty-one.

Chapter4

Mind Your Manners: Castiglione and *The Courtier*

No More Eating with Your Fingers

Before the Renaissance, back during the Middle Ages, no one would have been offended if you ate with your hands, talked with your mouth full, used your sleeve as a napkin, and let out a hearty burp at the end of the meal. Back then, silverware as we know it didn't even exist.

Maybe you're thinking, "Yuck! That's disgusting!" Or perhaps, "So I could eat *spaghetti* with my fingers? Cool!"

Sorry, but during the Renaissance this kind of fun came to an end. People rediscovered good manners. Or maybe it's more accurate to say they came up with a new set of rules. Men wrote pages and pages on the topic. Everyone wanted to behave in a way that showed his good breeding and reflected his noble background.

Castiglione

In the early 1500s, Baldassare Castiglione [ball-das-SAH-ray ka-stee-lee-OH-nay] wrote *The Book of the Courtier*. It's usually called *The Courtier* for short. In great detail, the book describes how the ideal courtier should behave.

What's a Courtier?

You see the word "court" in courtier? You know about the kind of court where trials take place with a judge and sometimes a jury. But this is a different kind of court—the court of a king or prince. When you refer to a prince's court, you might mean the palace or mansion where the prince lives. The court also includes the royal family, servants, officers, and advisers of the prince.

Some members of the court of Ludovico Gonzaga

So, a *courtier* is a person who spends a lot of time at the court of the prince. Sometimes, when people think of a courtier, they think of a person who hangs around the prince and flatters him and tries to gain his favor. But this stereotype does't apply to all courtiers.

The Well-Rounded Courtier

The Book of the Courtier describes the right ways to behave, but it's more than a book of manners. It describes what some people in the Renaissance thought of as an ideal type of person.

Castiglione said that a lady should be "witty, elegant, and cultured." He said a gentleman should be loyal to his prince and courteous to women. The courtier should be "athletic, sensitive, artistic, and well-educated."

A perfect courtier should be able to do everything well: he should be a skilled horseman, a bold soldier in battle, a graceful dancer, and more. He should be "well built and shapely of limb," not too short or too tall. And he should be a remarkable athlete: he should excel in jousting, wrestling, tennis, and spear-throwing! But, said Castiglione, the courtier should avoid some activities, "such as turning somersaults, rope-walking, and the like, which savor of the mountebank and little befit a gentleman." ("Savor of the mountebank" means "are suited to a clown.")

You might think that a courtier who can do everything well would be pretty conceited. But it's important, Castiglione said, to be "gentle, modest, and reserved." In other words, don't be a show-off.

Most important of all, the courtier "must accompany his actions, gestures, habits, in short his every movement, with grace." Even when the courtier is doing something very difficult, he should do it so gracefully that it looks easy. The Italian word for this quality is *sprezzatura* [spretz-zah-TOOR-ah]. It means the ability to make things look easy, as though you hardly have to try or think about what you're doing. In the language of today, we might say that the key to being a courtier is, "Never let them see you sweat!"

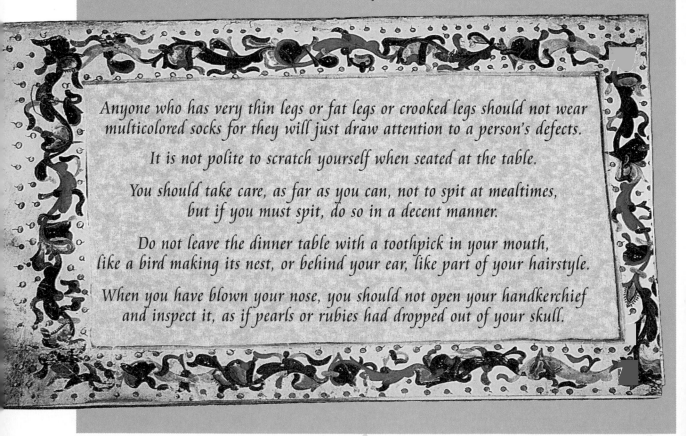

"If you must spit… "

A man named Giovanni della Casa wrote about proper behavior, too. Here are some tidbits of advice he sent to his nephew:

Anyone who has very thin legs or fat legs or crooked legs should not wear multicolored socks for they will just draw attention to a person's defects.

It is not polite to scratch yourself when seated at the table.

You should take care, as far as you can, not to spit at mealtimes, but if you must spit, do so in a decent manner.

Do not leave the dinner table with a toothpick in your mouth, like a bird making its nest, or behind your ear, like part of your hairstyle.

When you have blown your nose, you should not open your handkerchief and inspect it, as if pearls or rubies had dropped out of your skull.

Chapter 5

A woman's head, as sketched by a man—Leonardo da Vinci

What About Those Renaissance Women?

"A Light Thing and Vain"

What about the women of the Renaissance? Where were they? What were they doing?

Renaissance women inspired writers to create poetry, sculptors to fashion statues, and artists to paint beautiful portraits. Mostly, however, the sculptor's chisel and the painter's brush were kept out of the women's hands.

Although Renaissance men believed they could do almost anything, they didn't think the same of women. A merchant from Florence expressed the attitude of some of the men in his day. "A woman," he said, "is a light thing and vain.... If you have women in the house, keep them shut up and return often to keep them in fear and trembling." Nice guy.

Men of the Renaissance believed that a young woman born into a noble, wealthy family had three duties. (1) She should marry a rich man from an important family. (2) She should be loyal to that husband. And, (3) she should give him sons. When a son was born, everyone congratulated the mother. But if a daughter was born, people would smile politely and whisper, "Better luck next time."

Marriages to Keep the Peace

In Renaissance days, men and women did not date each other, fall in love, and then get married. (No one began to think that way about romance and marriage until a couple hundred years later, in the late eighteenth and early nineteenth centuries.) During the Renaissance, in upper class families most marriages were arranged by parents, usually while the children were still young.

Fathers preferred that their daughters marry rich and powerful men from other city-states or countries. Were these dads trying to get rid of their trouble-making daughters? Not at all. When the daughter of a prince in one city-state married the son of a ruler in another city-state, the two families would be much less likely to go to war. With a son, daughter, and grandchildren between them, the two rulers would have too much in common to fight each other.

This practice of arranged political marriages became common all across Europe. After a while, it seemed as if most of the ruling families were related to each other.

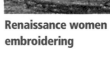

Renaissance women embroidering

The First Lady of the Renaissance

Although most Renaissance women were limited to running a household, embroidering, and dancing, some did manage to become powerful and influential despite all that stood in their way. One such woman was Isabella d'Este [d'ES-tay].

Isabella was born in the Italian city-state of Ferrara in 1474. Fortunately, her father, the Duke of Ferrara, believed in the importance of educating both his sons *and* his daughters.

Isabella blossomed into a brilliant student. When she was only six years old, she knew Latin and Greek, and played the lute (a popular instrument during the Renaissance, like a guitar). She was a feisty little girl who could and would debate anyone on any topic.

Other children called her "La Prima Donna" or "The First Lady." (You have to wonder if they were being a wee bit sarcastic.)

Engaged at Six!

The Duke of Ferrara believed in the strategic wisdom of arranged marriages. So, at the tender age of six years old, Isabella became engaged to Francesco Gonzaga of Mantua. But he was much older—all of fourteen!

The wedding took place when Isabella turned sixteen, a normal age in those times for a girl to get married. This marriage caused Isabella to be related to many ruling families in Italy.

After Isabella moved to Mantua, she wasted no time getting involved in the politics of the city. Francesco was often away, fighting one battle after another with various city-states and countries. When Francesco was out of town, Isabella competently governed the people.

In 1509, while Francesco was leading troops against the city of Venice, he was captured and put in jail for several years. With Francesco gone, it might seem like a good opportunity to the princes of unfriendly city-states to try to take over Mantua. But Isabella made it clear to potential enemies that she was very much in charge and they had better not try anything. While Francesco was in prison, she managed to fight off enemies and form strong alliances with other rulers.

Was Francesco grateful? No. Instead of thanking his wife, he complained, "It is our fate to have as a wife a woman who is always ruled by the head."

Once released from jail, Isabella's husband left to fight more battles. He fought against the French for a few years, and died in 1519.

After that, Isabella led Mantua on her own. She kept her enemies out and made certain that both Mantua and her home city of Ferrara stayed independent and unharmed.

A Passion for the Arts

Not only was Isabella an outstanding ruler, she was also a great patron of the arts. She collected antiques, rare books, and all types of artwork.

Tucked away in the Castle of St. George in Mantua, Isabella d'Este built a special room. She called it her *Grotta*, which means "cave." This treasure chamber contained the works of many of the great artists of the day. Gorgeous paintings hung on the walls of the Grotta. In beautifully carved wooden cabinets she kept ancient coins and medals, precious jewels and gemstones, exquisite vases, old manuscripts, and pieces of gold and silver.

Sculptors, writers, and painters visited Isabella's home often. She employed many of them. In fact, for many years she tried to persuade the great Leonardo da Vinci to paint her portrait. All she could get him to do was a quick sketch. At one point, he made the excuse that he was too busy working out geometry problems to stop and paint.

Finally, Isabella paid another great Renaissance artist, Titian [TISH-un], to capture her likeness on canvas. Titian did *too* precise a job. His portrait accurately portrayed Isabella, who was sixty years old at the time. When she looked at the picture, Isabella became furious and demanded that he re-paint it. On his second try, Titian wisely made Isabella look a good twenty years younger!

Isabella didn't forget her fellow women, either. She started a school where young girls could learn Greek, Latin, the arts, philosophy, and literature.

Isabella was an unusual woman for her time. She is justly remembered as the "First Lady of the Renaissance."

Titian's second portrait of Isabella d'Este

While Titian was much in demand to paint portraits, he became famous for his powerful and boldly colored paintings of scenes from the Bible and from classical mythology. Many people consider Titian the greatest Venetian painter of the sixteenth century.

Chapter 6

Leonardo da Vinci: The Complete Renaissance Man

In this detail from Verrocchio's *Baptism of Christ*, a young Leonardo painted the angel on the left.

An Amazing Apprentice

If you had to pick just one person to represent the spirit of the Renaissance, it would probably be Leonardo da Vinci. Painter, inventor, scientist, musician, and more, Leonardo is the embodiment of the belief that you can do anything you set your mind to.

He was born on April 15, 1452, in Vinci, a town near Florence. As a young boy, he worked as an apprentice to Andrea del Verrocchio [ahn-DREH-ah del vair-ROCK-kyo], the leading painter and sculptor of Florence. Leonardo's work as an apprentice kept him busy from dawn to dusk. He swept floors, fetched supplies, and made brushes. He also practiced drawing and painting each day. It didn't take long for people to notice Leonardo's artistic genius.

In those days, often a master artist would paint the main features of a picture but leave it for an apprentice to finish the landscape or other smaller figures in the background. In 1476, Verrocchio was working on a painting called The Baptism of Christ. Verrocchio painted one angel, then asked Leonardo to paint another. Legend has it that Leonardo's angel looked so much better than Verrocchio's that the old master never picked up a brush again.

Leonardo in Milan

When Leonardo was about thirty years old, he was invited to work for the

Duke of Milan, Lodovico Sforza. While he lived in Milan, Leonardo continued to make works of art, but the Duke also employed him as a military engineer. Although Leonardo called war "beastly madness," he designed some very dangerous weapons, including an early version of a tank.

When the Duke wanted to impress his fellow noblemen, he asked Leonardo to organize spectacular festivals. Leonardo took charge of designing costumes, creating fancy stage sets, and selecting the music.

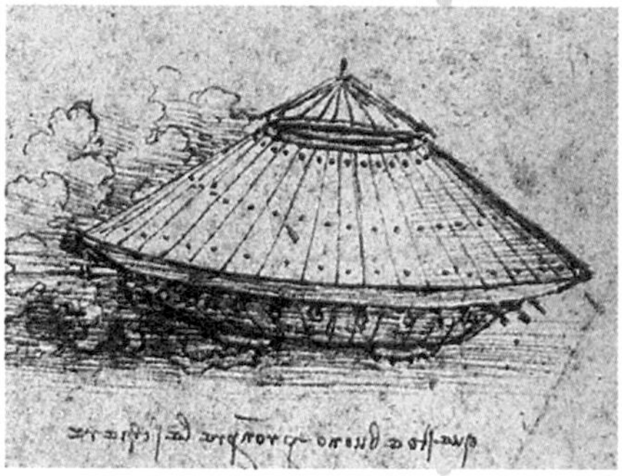

Leonardo sketched this idea for a tank.

Leonardo sketched various ideas for a huge monument in the shape of a horse.

While employed by the Duke of Milan, Leonardo constructed a huge monument made of terra cotta, a clay-like material. The monument was in the shape of a horse. The gigantic clay model was supposed to be cast in bronze. But the Duke wound up using the bronze to make weapons for war. Worse yet, French soldiers invading Milan used the clay horse for target practice and completely destroyed it.

Leonardo the Prankster

Do your parents hate to be interrupted when they are Thinking Deep Thoughts? Leonardo felt the same way. In fact, he played tricks on visitors who pestered him.

Leonardo took his large pet lizard and fastened a scary-looking horn to his head. Then, he strapped bat-like wings to the sides of the reptile and glued shiny spots on its skin. He kept the lizard in a big box in his studio.

When a person disturbed him, Leonardo would politely say something like, "I have the most fascinating object in my box. Would you care to see it?"

When Leonardo opened the box, his ferocious "dragon" would scurry across the room toward the unwanted guest. The terrified visitor usually ran out of the room screaming.

The Painter at Work: A Portrait and *The Last Supper*

In Milan Leonardo kept busy putting on pageants, trying to build a gigantic horse, designing weapons and machines, and even designing a whole new plan for the city. Did he ever find time to paint?

Yes, indeed. Look at the portrait called *Lady with an Ermine*. A less talented artist filled in the dark background, but you can see Leonardo's genius in the way the body of the animal curves, and in the amazing expressiveness of the lady's hand.

Lady with an Ermine

While he lived in Milan, Leonardo did one of his greatest paintings, *The Last Supper*. It shows the reaction of the twelve apostles as Jesus makes the shocking announcement, "One of you will betray me."

The twelve apostles [uh-POS-uls]: According to the New Testament, Jesus chose twelve of his closest followers to travel with him and learn directly from him. These "apostles" would later go out and teach others what Jesus had taught them. Some of their names were Simon Peter, James, John, Matthew, Thomas, and Judas.

How do you paint thirteen men at a table and still show all their faces and expressions? Leonardo decided to place the apostles in groups of three, with Jesus seated alone in the middle. Notice how Leonardo isolates the figure of Judas, the betrayer of Jesus. Judas leans far backward, away from Jesus.

Look at the expressions on the men's faces and their gestures, especially their expressive hands. Leonardo wandered the streets of Milan searching for exactly the right faces and right poses to use as models for the characters in this picture.

The Last Supper is painted on the wall of a dining hall in a monastery. While Leonardo worked on the painting, the head of the monastery, called the prior, became impatient for him to finish. He complained that Leonardo was lazy, and that the artist was spending too much time wandering the streets looking for the right face for Judas. Leonardo admitted that it was taking him a long time to find the right face for Judas. But, said Leonardo to the prior, "If you're in a great hurry, then I could always use your face."

It took Leonardo two years (from 1495 to 1497) to finish *The Last Supper*. The painting made Leonardo famous throughout Europe. Other artists and engravers made copies of it for centuries.

The Last Supper

But the painting itself did not last very long. Leonardo experimented with a new fresco technique, using oil and varnish mixed in with his colors. The paint absorbed the moisture from the wall and crumbled over time. Recently, artists who specialize in restoring old paintings have used advanced scientific techniques to try to make *The Last Supper* look more like what Leonardo painted.

Fresco **is the Italian word for fresh. It also refers to a technique of painting on a wall. An artist or his assistants applied fresh plaster to a small section of a wall. The artist painted on the damp plaster. As the paint dried, it was incorporated into the plaster and made a hard surface. Fresco painting required that an artist work quickly and paint only a small section at a time.**

Putting Things in Perspective

The Last Supper is painted on a wall about fourteen by thirty feet large. The wall, of course, is flat, but the painting seems to have depth. It almost seems as if you could walk through the open windows into the landscape in the background.

To create a sense of depth in a flat painting, Leonardo used the technique called *perspective*. Perspective was a new technique in the Renaissance. Before the Renaissance, most paintings looked flat and had no sense of depth. Perspective gave Renaissance painters an important new way to make their pictures look more real and lifelike.

Leonardo did not invent perspective. That honor is usually given to the Italian Renaissance artist and architect named Brunelleschi [broo-nuh-LESS-key]. (You'll read more about him in the next chapter of this book.)

Brunelleschi noticed that when we look at things, objects that are close look bigger, while those that are far away look smaller. He also noticed that if you stand between two parallel lines that stretch into the distance, the lines appear to come closer and closer together until they meet at a point on the horizon. When the lines come together, they seem to vanish, so this point is called the vanishing point.

In *The Last Supper*, Leonardo followed the rules of perspective when he painted the walls and the lines of the ceiling. If you were to extend the lines of the ceiling to the horizon, they would meet at a vanishing point in the center of the painting, somewhere behind the head of Jesus. Look at the diagram to see how the lines of the ceiling work in the painting. This draws your attention to Jesus as the most important figure in the painting.

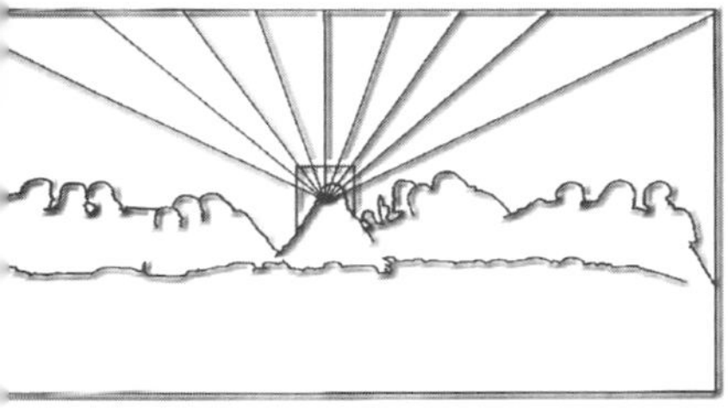

Notice also that Leonardo has put an open door and windows behind the figure of Jesus. Through them you can see the landscape in the distance. In a book he wrote on techniques of painting, Leonardo added some refinements to the use of perspective. He said that when you paint objects at a distance, you should not make them too detailed, and you should make the colors a little weaker. Have you noticed that's how faraway things appear in life?

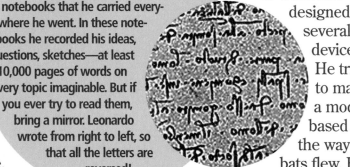

Leonardo's Backward Handwriting

Leonardo constantly wrote in the notebooks that he carried everywhere he went. In these notebooks he recorded his ideas, questions, sketches—at least 10,000 pages of words on every topic imaginable. But if you ever try to read them, bring a mirror. Leonardo wrote from right to left, so that all the letters are reversed!

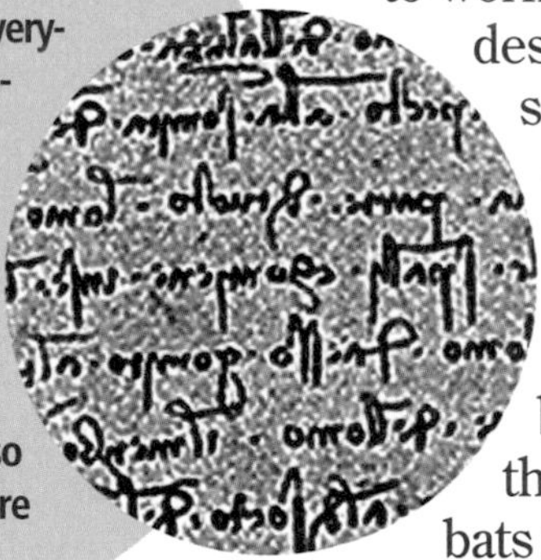

Leonardo the Scientist

After he left the city of Milan, Leonardo lived in several places, including his beloved city of Florence. For a while he worked for Cesare Borgia as a map maker and military engineer, and he became friends with Machiavelli.

Leonardo anticipated how helicopters fly in this sketch of an airscrew.

In 1506, Leonardo returned to Milan. As time went on, he became more interested in science than in art. In fact, at one point he wrote that he "could not bear the sight of a paintbrush."

When Leonardo looked at the sky and saw birds soaring gracefully through the air, he wondered, "How can man fly, too?" Being Leonardo, he got to work and designed several devices. He tried to make a model based on the way bats flew. He boarded up the windows of the room he worked in so that no one would know if his flying machine failed.

It didn't work. Still, Leonardo's attempts were far from total failures. In the course of his studies, he developed some of the basic ideas for both parachutes and helicopters.

Leonardo explored almost every field of science, including optics,

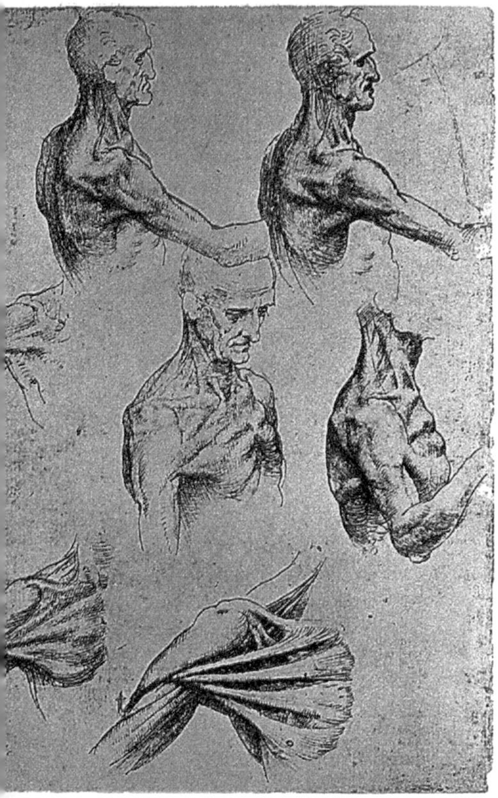

Leonardo made many anatomical drawings.

geology, botany, physics, and engineering. He made great advances in the study of anatomy. His notebooks are filled with highly detailed drawings of human bodies—not just the outside, but the insides, too. He dissected over thirty cadavers, until the pope commanded him to stay out of the morgue.

Take a look at a famous drawing that Leonardo made of the body. The picture is now known as *The Proportions of Man*. Wait a minute—didn't Leonardo know that human beings only have two arms and two legs? Of course. Leonardo created this diagram for a special purpose: to show how the proportions of human form relate to the laws of geometry.

For this drawing, Leonardo borrowed some ideas from a Roman architect named Vitruvius [vih-TROO-vee-us]. Vitruvius said that if a perfectly proportioned man stretched out on his back with his arms and legs extended, his belly button would be at the center of a circle. His fingers and toes would just touch the edge of the circle.

If that same perfectly proportioned man kept his legs together and stretched his arms out horizontally, his fingers and toes would touch the edges of a square. Leonardo used these guidelines to draw *The Proportions of Man*.

Are You Smiling at Me?

While Leonardo lived in Milan for the second time, he painted what may be the most famous painting of all time. It's a portrait called the *Mona Lisa*, yet no one knows the identity of the woman in the picture. Some say she was the

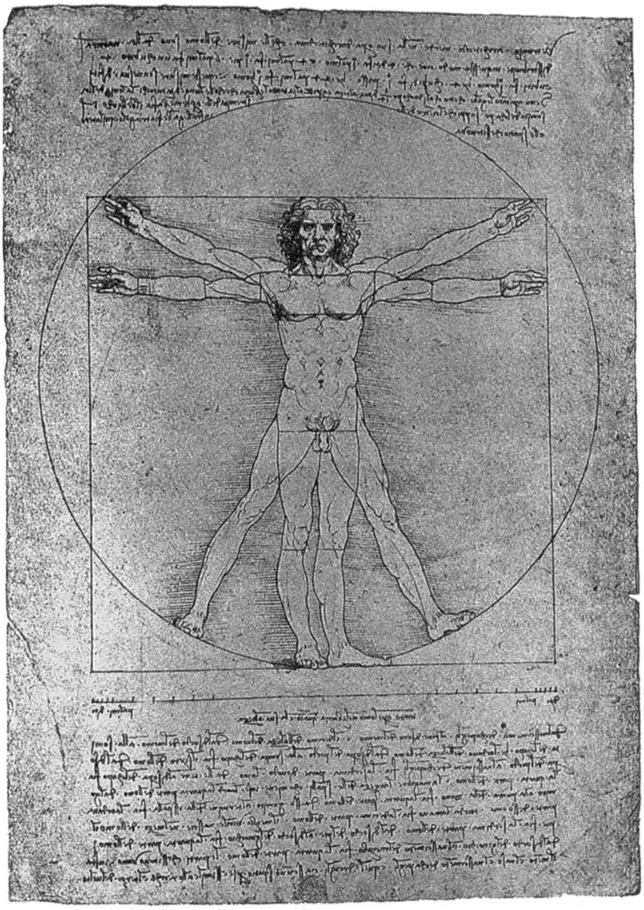

The Proportions of Man

Mona Lisa

wife of a wealthy man of Florence. Others claim she was a lady from Naples. Still others think she was a widowed duchess.

For hundreds of years, people have been fascinated by the *Mona Lisa*. Look at the way she smiles. In a book called *Lives of the Artists,* a Renaissance painter and writer named Giorgio Vasari [JOR-joe vah-ZAH-ree] wrote, "While Leonardo was painting Mona Lisa, he engaged musicians who played and jested and so he drew forth that smile so pleasing." But that doesn't quite explain everything in her expression. What is she thinking behind that smile? What is she looking at? Is she looking *at* you or *around* you?

Leonardo added to the mystery of the *Mona Lisa* by painting an unusual, misty-looking landscape in the back-ground. Here's a special artistic term that will impress your friends: if you

The Age of Exploration

In Europe, the Renaissance was not only a time of artistic rebirth but also a great age of exploration. While artists and scholars were rediscovering the classics, explorers were discovering the "New World." It was "new," at least, to the Europeans, because before 1492 most of them did not know that North and South America existed.

Quick quiz: Who was it that, on October 12, 1492, landed on an island that he thought was part the East Indies, south of China? It turned out that he had in fact landed on an island in the Bahamas, not far from what is now Florida. (It was, of course, Christopher Columbus.)

Before the fifteenth century, Europeans did not sail very far from their own shores. But beginning in the fifteenth century, many ships set sail from Portugal, Spain, the Netherlands, and England. The men on these ships hoped to achieve different goals. Some wanted to grow rich from trade in gold, silks, and spices. Some wanted to spread Christianity. Some wanted to claim the lands they found and set up colonies—which often led to violent conflict with the native people already living on the lands the Europeans claimed.

During the lifetime of Leonardo da Vinci, Columbus reached the "New World," Vasco da Gama sailed around the Cape of Good Hope to India, and Ferdinand Magellan set out on the first journey around the world. (Magellan was killed before the voyage ended, but his ship did make it back to Spain.)

look closely, you will notice that Leonardo uses a technique called *sfumato* [sfoo-MAH-toe]. Sfumato is a way of painting that creates smooth changes between different areas of color and shading in a picture. The end result is a soft, hazy, smokey look—the perfect background for this mysterious woman!

Leonardo lived in troubled times. When fighting broke out again in Milan, he moved to Rome and worked for Pope Leo X. But the pope seemed to favor other artists of the day. So, when King Francis I invited him to France, Leonardo left Italy, never to return. He advised the French king on many architectural projects before he died in 1519.

The next time you hear the term "Renaissance Man," think of Leonardo da Vinci, a man whose boundless curiosity, multiple talents, and visionary imagination summed up the spirit of the times.

A self-portrait by Leonardo, drawn when he was about sixty years old

Chapter7

Three from the Early Renaissance

Before Leonardo

Leonardo da Vinci wasn't the first important Renaissance artist. He comes first in this book because he was, in so many ways, the complete Renaissance man.

Other important artists came before Leonardo. They did much of their work during what some historians call the Early Renaissance—about the first half of the fifteenth century.

What an exciting time to be alive, especially if you were an artist living in Florence! Painters, sculptors, architects, and philosophers were busy and buzzing with ideas. All of them studied and talked about classical works. With help from wealthy families like the Medicis, they created splendid projects, building on each other's skills and creativity.

Let's meet three of these artists: an architect, a sculptor, and a painter.

Brunelleschi Loses

Before Filippo Brunelleschi [broo-nuh-LESS-key] devoted himself to architecture, he worked as a goldsmith. In 1402, when the city council of Florence invited artists to submit ideas for decorating the huge doors of the Baptistery (a place where people were baptized), Brunelleschi created a beautiful design.

Ghiberti designed these doors for the Florence Baptistery.

But his design didn't win. The winning design was submitted by Lorenzo Ghiberti [ghee-BARE-tee]. When Ghiberti found out that he'd won, he bragged, "I have surpassed everyone."

The Florence city council offered to allow Brunelleschi to work as Ghiberti's assistant. But Ghiberti flatly refused his help. This started a bitter lifelong rivalry between the men.

Brunelleschi made a great advance when he developed the mathematical rules for perspective, a way of showing depth on a flat paper. Do you remember how Leonardo da Vinci used perspective in his great painting, *The Last Supper*? (See page 34 in this book.)

After losing the contest, Brunelleschi decided to explore his interests in architecture. In the spirit of the Renaissance, he rejected the Middle Ages and the Gothic style. Instead, he looked back to classical times. He studied the ruins of Roman buildings. He loved their simplicity. He admired the strong, straight columns and graceful arches.

Brunelleschi admired the classical architecture of buildings like the Roman Temple of the Sun.

Brunelleschi Wins

As the years passed, Brunelleschi took what he learned from the ancient Romans and began to develop his own ideas about architecture. Those ideas came in handy when, in 1418, the Guild of Wool Merchants in Florence announced another competition. They wanted to find someone who could solve a very difficult architectural problem: how to put a roof over a *huge* space.

The space was over the middle of a cathedral. Work had begun on the cathedral eighty years before Brunelleschi was born, but it still wasn't finished. The plans called for a roof to be placed over the middle of the church, an area 136 feet wide. Even if the builders could find trees to make boards long enough to span the space, the roof would certainly cave in on itself under the tremendous weight.

For years, the architects of Florence had been arguing about how to build this roof. Some people said it was impossible. But Brunelleschi confidently approached the Wool Merchants and announced that he could do it. How? By covering the space with a dome.

When the guild members demanded to see his plans, Brunelleschi refused. He claimed they would steal his ideas and give the work to other architects.

To illustrate his point, Brunelleschi brought an egg to a guild meeting. Imagine you are a guild member at this meeting. You hear Brunelleschi ask, "Can any one of you make this egg stand on its head without toppling?"

No one replies. So, Brunelleschi cracks the egg on the table and balances it on its jagged top. One of your fellow guild members sneers, "We could have done that!"

But Brunelleschi responds, "That's precisely my point. If I tell you my plans to build the dome, you'll say you knew how to do it all along."

In the end, Brunelleschi convinced the guild members, and they chose him undertake the project. But then the Wool Merchants got cold feet. They weren't so sure Brunelleschi

During the Middle Ages, masons had to carry their bricks and other heavy materials to great heights when they worked on cathedrals. Brunelleschi made the workers lives much safer by inventing a hoisting machine with pulleys. The masons could use the machine to haul items up to the high scaffold where they worked.

The Florence Cathedral, with the dome designed by Brunelleschi

could successfully do the job on his own. They thought he needed someone to help him with such a difficult task. So they picked Brunelleschi's old rival, Ghiberti.

Brunelleschi was steaming mad. He knew Ghiberti had no idea how to build the dome. So Brunelleschi pretended to be sick. While he lay in bed for days, all work stopped. Finally, messengers came to Brunelleschi. They told him that Ghiberti could do nothing without him, and they begged him to come back.

The clever architect made his point. From then on, Brunelleschi alone was in charge.

As all of Florence watched, Brunelleschi accomplished a stunning architectural feat: the building of the dome of the Florence Cathedral.

Brunelleschi solved the architectural problem by constructing the dome out of two thin shells of bricks. The inner shell supported the outer shell and prevented the dome from collapsing in on itself. To further strengthen the dome, Brunelleschi added curved ribs which extended from the top of the cathedral walls to the bottom of the tip of the dome.

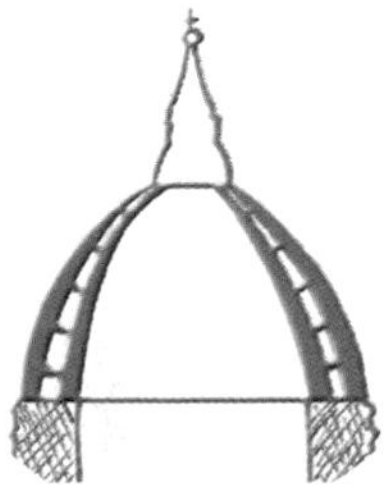

An inner shell supports the outer shell.

They said it couldn't be done, but Brunelleschi did it!

Donatello the Sculptor

The greatest sculptor of the Early Renaissance went by the name of Donatello [don-uh-TEL-oh]. As a young man, he helped Lorenzo Ghiberti decorate the doors of the Baptistery in Florence. Later, Donatello worked with Ghiberti's rival, Brunelleschi. Scholars believe that Donatello and Brunelleschi visited Rome together to study the ancient ruins.

Donatello drew from all these experiences when he created his well-known sculpture, *St. George*. On the rectangular base of the statue, Donatello

Donatello's *St. George*

carved a scene from the popular legend in which St. George battles a dragon. According to the legend, there was once a fierce dragon terrorizing a town. The people gave the dragon sheep, but the dragon demanded human sacrifices. The unlucky victims were chosen by lottery. When the daughter of the king was chosen, she went to meet her fate. But St. George arrived just in time to save the princess and kill the dragon. Before leaving the scene, he also converted all the townspeople to Christianity.

The standing figure of St. George that Donatello carved is a proud and confident warrior. His strong, muscular form shows through his armor. His watchful eyes and his slightly turned stance make him seem ready for whatever challenges may come his way. In this strong, watchful warrior, the people of Florence must have seen the embodiment of their own spirit.

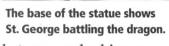

The base of the statue shows St. George battling the dragon.

A Little Barrel?

Alessandro di Mariano Filipepi was his real name, but he was called Sandro Botticelli [bot-ih-CHEL-ee]. "Botticelli" means "little barrel" in Italian. As far as we know, the nickname was first applied to Botticelli's older brother, and, when young Sandro went to live with him, people started calling him Botticelli too. While the nickname doesn't bring graceful images to mind, Botticelli's paintings are known for their grace, elegance, and beauty.

Botticelli's most famous painting shows a scene from classical mythology. In *The Birth of Venus*, the goddess of love seems to float on a shell on the sea. Botticelli painted Venus in a pose from an ancient Roman statue, then added his own touches such as the flowing hair and the almost sad expression. The wind gods blow gentle breezes to move the goddess ashore, where a flowered robe is ready to cover her.

Botticelli was one of Lorenzo de' Medici's favorite painters, but his

The Birth of Venus

association with the Medicis ended when the family left Florence after Lorenzo's death. Botticelli lost much of his financial support, too. Do you remember that, after the Medicis left Florence, the monk Savonarola took charge? Savonarola did not approve of paintings like *The Birth of Venus.* He said such paintings were part of a "cult of paganism."

This is simply scandalous!

What Savonarola thought of Botticelli

Savonarola's severe sermons must have affected Botticelli deeply. He stopped painting scenes from classical mythology and turned his attention to religious themes. For example, instead of painting Venus, he painted Mary, the mother of Jesus. But he still painted her with grace and elegance.

Chapter8

Michelangelo: An Artist for All Seasons

Playing Hooky for Art

One day, a group of boys were called to the home of Lorenzo de' Medici. What could a man so rich and powerful, a man people called "the Magnificent," want to tell these boys?

Lorenzo looked at the boys and made an announcement. "You see this stone figure?" he said, pointing to an ancient Roman statue of a nature god called a faun. "A brilliant sculptor created this piece centuries ago. I want each of you to carve a statue exactly like this one."

Some of the boys groaned. Lorenzo paid no attention. "Work quickly and accurately," he said. "The young man who produces the best sculpture wins a place in my art school."

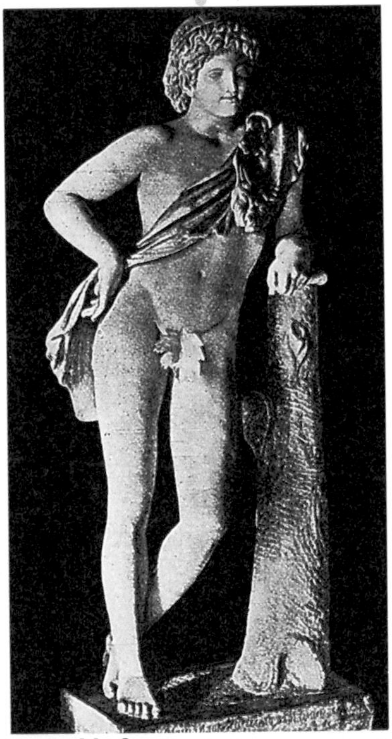
A marble faun

Some time later, as Lorenzo strolled through his courtyard, he spotted one boy whose work looked far superior to the rest. He turned to his assistant and asked, "Who is that child? Look at how he has carved the head of the faun. It's difficult to tell his work from the real thing!"

The assistant checked his list. "Let's see. Michelangelo Buonarotti [mye-kul-AN-juh-low bwahn-uh-ROW-tee], second son of a former small-town mayor. Family is from minor nobility. Mother died when the boy was six. Hmm . . . not a very good Latin or Greek scholar. Ran away from school a lot."

"Ran away?"

"Yes, it seems he sneaked away from school to go to the churches, where he spent hours copying the paintings."

"Ah, a true art lover," said Lorenzo.

"Well, his father isn't. The boy came home to many a beating. Even now, the father's upset that Michelangelo works as an apprentice in Ghirlandaio's [geer-lahn-DAH-yo] studio. He thinks it's beneath the family's dignity for the boy to dirty his hands with such work."

Lorenzo walked up to Michelangelo and gazed at the faun's head the boy had carved. "That's a lovely sculpture," Lorenzo commented. Then he said, "Young man, come live in our home and learn what you can from us."

Lorenzo's invitation was a great honor, but Michelangelo's father wasn't thrilled. He changed his mind, however, when Lorenzo offered him a job and gave Michelangelo a beautiful cloak and a handsome sum of money.

In the Medici household, Michelangelo discussed art and literature with the finest minds of the time. He studied the old masters in sculpture and painting. His stay with the Medicis launched his career in the art world.

Michelangelo Made It—and Don't You Forget It!

On a stormy night in 1492, Lorenzo de' Medici died. The sudden loss shocked the people of Florence. Michelangelo, in particular, lost a friend and a patron, a man who had recognized the young artist's genius and supported him in his efforts. Lorenzo's son, Piero "the Unlucky," was no friend of Michelangelo or the arts. When he took over, he brought hard times to Florence. Reluctantly, Michelangelo left his beloved city.

After some years of moving here and there, Michelangelo went to Rome. In Rome, a church official who had heard about the young sculptor's work offered him a large payment. He told Michelangelo to create something spectacular so that people would remember him when he was gone.

The church official wanted Michelangelo to carve what is called a *pietà* [pyay-TAH; the first syllable rhymes with "play"]. *Pietà* is an Italian word that means "pity" or "mercy." In art, *pietà* refers to a painting or sculpture that shows the Virgin Mary mourning over the dead body of Jesus.

Michelangelo's *Pietà*

Twenty-four-year-old Michelangelo got to work immediately. In less than twelve months, he carved the stunningly beautiful *Pietà*. The sculpture shows the Virgin Mary holding Jesus across her lap just after He was removed from the cross.

The *Pietà* was placed in the great church of the Vatican in Rome, St. Peter's Basilica. Once, when Michelangelo went to St. Peter's to look at his creation, a group of visitors stood in front of it trying to guess who carved the amazing work. They guessed it was an artist nicknamed "The Hunchback" who lived in an outlying city.

That didn't make Michelangelo happy. Later, in the middle of the night, he returned to the Basilica with hammer and chisel in hand. So there would be no question in the future, he carved these words on the sash that runs diagonally across Mary: "MICHELANGELO BUONARROTI THE FLORENTINE MADE IT." As far as anyone knows, this is the only piece of art Michelangelo ever signed.

How did sculptors create such magnificent forms from raw hunks of stone?
Here is one technique they used:

1. **Make sketches to work out just how the figures will be placed.**
2. **Carve a wax or clay model of the sculpture, so you can see how it looks in three dimensions.**
3. **Lay the wax or clay figure lengthwise in a long vat of water that completely covers the model.**
4. **Lower the water level little by little. The parts of the model that appear first are the parts you carve first on the stone.**

Eventually, the form seems to release itself from the marble. Sound easy? It's not!

From the Giant Comes the Giant Slayer

The *Pietà* made Michelangelo the most famous sculptor in Italy. In 1501, he returned to Florence. There, officials of the cathedral showed Michelangelo a huge rectangular block of marble known as "the Giant." They showed him where a so-called artist had begun to work on the huge block but then made a mess of it. Then they challenged Michelangelo: Can you make something out of this?

Michelangelo accepted the challenge. From the twenty-foot block, he set out to carve a huge statue of David, the biblical hero who had used his slingshot to slay the giant enemy, Goliath.

The people of Florence loved the idea of a statue of David. The story of David reminded them of their own small city, bravely overcoming difficulties as they resisted the "giants" threatening them—other city-states and foreign countries looking to take over.

It took Michelangelo two and a half years to complete his statue of David. The figure stood almost fourteen feet high and weighed 11,000 pounds. Like ancient Greek statues, Michelangelo's *David* shows a strong, muscular human form, almost a picture of perfection, a figure full of power and grace. This is no smiling boy but a thoughtful young man with an intense, watchful expression.

In his book, *Lives of the Artists*, Giorgio Vasari wrote, "Anyone who has seen Michelangelo's *David* has no need to see anything else by any other sculptor, living or dead."

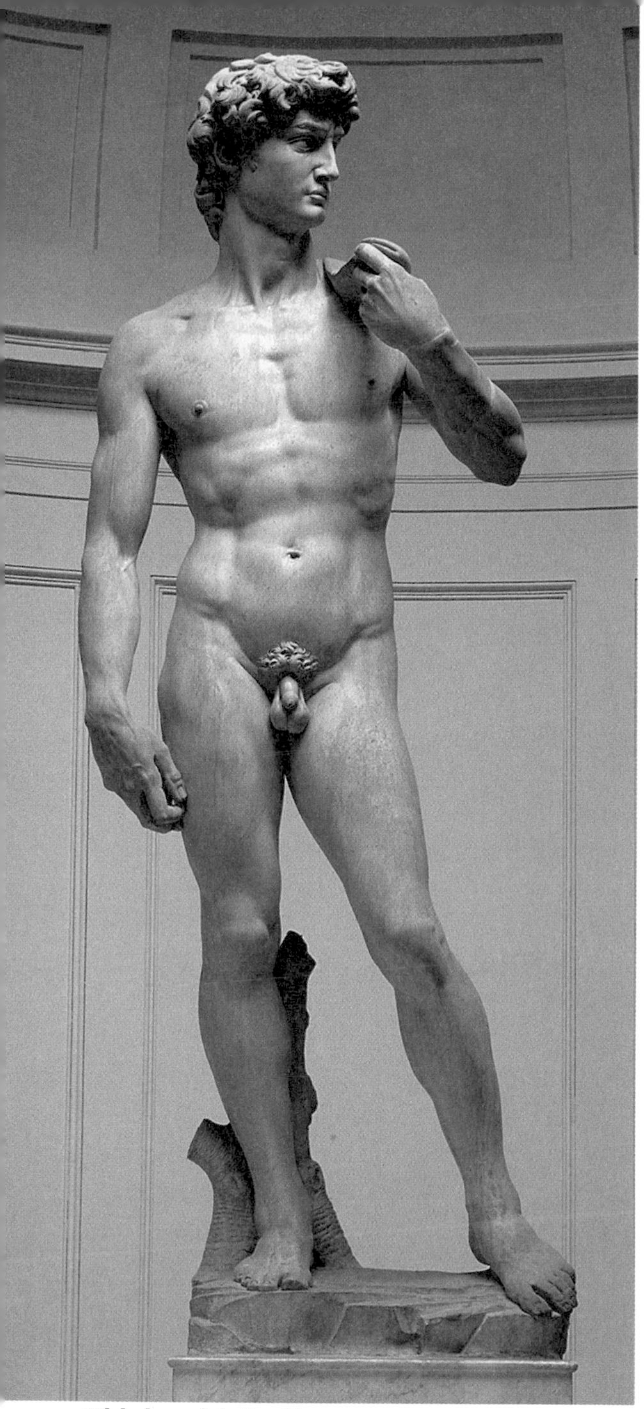

Michelangelo's *David*

Julius II and Michelangelo: A Stormy Relationship

Do you remember Julius II, the "warrior pope"? (See page 18.) He was the pope who wanted to acquire as much art as possible to glorify the church.

Julius II was a man of great ambition, determination, and energy. When his mind was made up, you wouldn't want to be in his way. And, he had a terrible temper. In other words, he was a lot like Michelangelo. So, when these two powerful personalities came together, sparks were bound to fly.

Julius asked Michelangelo to construct a colossal tomb for him that would be built under the dome of St. Peter's Basilica. Julius was not modest—he wanted to be sure people remembered him. He wanted a massive tomb that would be surrounded by forty marble figures.

Michelangelo set to work hauling in tons of stone from the cliffs of Carrara, a place where he spent his childhood. After great labor and expense, Michelangelo filled the town square with blocks of marble.

But then Julius lost interest and gave an order to stop work on the project. Some historians think that other artists who had been employed by the pope, and who were jealous of Michelangelo, might have had something to do with it.

Whatever happened, Julius refused to pay Michelangelo or even talk with him. An angry Michelangelo packed his bags and headed back to Florence. An even angrier Julius sent a messenger to demand that Michelangelo return to Rome. Michelangelo told the messenger he would return when the pope paid what he owed him and stuck to his promises.

Workers haul blocks of marble cut from the cliffs of Carrara.

"Where are his clothes?"

The picture here shows the Apollo Belvedere, an ancient Roman sculpture of Apollo, the god of light, music, and poetry. Like many works of art from ancient Greece and Rome, the Apollo Belvedere is a nude. In art, a nude is a human figure without any clothes. Classical artists saw beauty in the healthy human body, and often depicted the naked body in their works.

Apollo Belvedere

During the Middle Ages, nudity was not common in art, since the church considered nakedness shameful. But in the Renaissance, Michelangelo and others revived the classical ideal of the nude as a proper subject for art. The Renaissance artists were inspired by classical sculptures, which they saw as models of beauty, grace, and strength.

Did the pope apologize and pay Michelangelo, and did everyone live happily ever after? Definitely not! Julius sent furious commands to the leaders of Florence: Send Michelangelo back to Rome, said the pope, or I will come get him with my armies if necessary.

A Florentine leader who was also a friend of Michelangelo suggested he return to Rome. After all, he told the angry artist, Florence did not wish to have to go to war for Michelangelo's sake!

It took months, but eventually Michelangelo did go back to Rome. When he got there, the pope had a job waiting for him. The pope had decided that the tomb could wait. Instead, he wanted Michelangelo to paint the ceiling of the Sistine Chapel.

Michelangelo refused: I am a sculptor, not a painter, he told the pope. And the ceiling itself was immense—a huge, high, curved surface covering more than 5,800 square feet (about twice as big as a tennis court!).

Michelangelo urged the pope to give the job to someone else. But the pope insisted. And insisted again. And kept insisting until Michelangelo reluctantly agreed.

Painting the Sistine Ceiling

Years before, when he worked as an apprentice, Michelangelo had learned the technique of fresco painting. Remember, in fresco painting the artist applies a coat of wet plaster to a surface, then paints on the plaster. The idea is that the paint will soak into the plaster. As the paint and plaster dry together, the painting will become a permanent part of the wall, or in this case, the ceiling.

Michelangelo prepared to start the monumental task of painting the ceiling of the Sistine Chapel. From the beginning, he and the pope argued. Julius wanted the ceiling to portray the twelve apostles. Michelangelo wanted to paint something grander and more dynamic, a group of scenes from the Old Testament, from the biblical story of Creation to the story of Moses. This time, Michelangelo got his way.

At first, Michelangelo got help from several Florentine painters. But one by

The Creation of Adam: **In this detail from the ceiling of the Sistine Chapel, Michelangelo painted the moment, described in the book of Genesis in the Bible, when God gives life to Adam. You can also see Eve (according to Genesis, the first woman), yet to be born, protected under God's left arm.**

one he sent them away. He was a perfectionist—no one could meet his standards but himself.

So he had to complete the grueling work on his own. From a scaffold high above the floor, Michelangelo had to bend and reach to paint the ceiling above his head. His neck and back ached terribly; his eyes grew strained. Paint splattered down on him: "My beard points to heaven," he wrote, and "my paint-brush all the day does drop a rich mosaic on my face." Day and night, week after week, month after month, he kept painting.

If he asks me one more time, I'm going to drop this bucket of plaster on his head!
When will you finish?

Pope Julius didn't make life any easier. He constantly urged Michelangelo to hurry. Every day, the pope shouted up at the artist: When will you finish?! Every day, Michelangelo answered: When I can! Once, when Michelangelo asked for time off to visit his family, Julius struck the artist with a cane. Another time, the pope threatened to throw Michelangelo off the scaffold if he didn't finish soon.

Finally, in October of 1512, after almost four and a half years of work, Michelangelo completed the ceiling. Great crowds hurried to the Vatican. They gazed in wonder at the ceiling and claimed, Michelangelo is not just the greatest sculptor of our time, he is the greatest painter as well.

Only four months later, Pope Julius II

This picture shows part of *The Last Judgment*.

died. The pope never did get his colossal tomb in St. Peter's. He was laid to rest in a smaller tomb in a smaller church, though the tomb was still a big and magnificent work of art. Michelangelo worked on it, on and off, for more than thirty years.

Michelangelo's Later Years

Compared to most men of his time, Michelangelo lived a very long life. For many years after the death of Julius II, he stayed busy and creative, working not only on Julius's tomb but on other sculptures and paintings.

One great achievement in these later years was another painting in the Sistine Chapel. On the altar wall, he painted *The Last Judgment*, mixing scenes from the Bible with classical mythology. He painted Christ, the Virgin Mary, saints, and angels. He painted the mythological figure of Charon, who ferries condemned souls across the river Styx to the dark underworld.

When Michelangelo painted the Last Judgment, none of the figures was clothed. An important clergyman of the time objected. He said that a sacred work of art should not contain nudity.

Michelangelo didn't see any conflict between the classical ideal of nudity in art and his own religious faith. Michelangelo painted the face of the church official who criticized him on the

The dome of St. Peter's

The dome of the U. S. Capitol

character Minos, the judge of the underworld. For good measure, he also added a donkey's ears and serpent's tail to the figure. However, the people in the painting did not stay naked for long. After Michelangelo's death, the church went through great changes and became much more conservative. Church officials hired an artist to paint clothing on all the nudes.

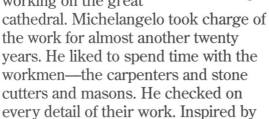

In his later years, Michelangelo turned out to be a great architect. He took over as chief architect of St. Peter's Basilica. For more than forty years, architects and engineers had been working on the great cathedral. Michelangelo took charge of the work for almost another twenty years. He liked to spend time with the workmen—the carpenters and stone cutters and masons. He checked on every detail of their work. Inspired by Brunelleschi's dome for the Florence Cathedral, Michelangelo designed a splendid dome for St. Peter's. His design has been copied for domes on buildings in many countries, including the United States Capitol building in Washington, D.C.

Michelangelo

One rainy winter day, when Michelangelo was eighty-nine years old, he climbed on a horse and took a ride through the Roman countryside. When he returned home he felt feverish. A few days later, he died.

The citizens of Rome insisted that he be buried in their city. But Michelangelo had wished otherwise. So, in the dark of night, Michelangelo's nephew hid the great artist's body and conveyed him to Florence, where he could rest in peace in the city he called home.

Chapter9

Raphael the Painter

Notice how Raphael uses perspective in this painting called *Marriage of the Virgin.* In the foreground, we see a group of people including Mary, Joseph, and the guests at the wedding. In the background, under the arches of the building, other people are standing, but they are painted much smaller, which makes them seem farther away and so gives the painting a feeling of depth.

"The Big Three"

If you had to name "The Big Three" among Italian Renaissance artists, you'd certainly include Leonardo da Vinci and Michelangelo. And the third, many people would agree, would be the artist known as Raphael.

He was born Raffaello Sanzio in 1483. He was younger than both Leonardo and Michelangelo, though Michelangelo lived longer. Raphael lost both of his parents at an early age. By eleven, he was on his own, working as an apprentice in a busy art studio. It didn't take long for him to establish a reputation for himself. Even as a young man, he was capable of painting a masterpiece like the *Marriage of the Virgin*.

Were Leonardo, Michelangelo, and Raphael friends? No—in fact, they were rivals and competitors. They may have admired each other's work, but they had almost nothing good to say about each other. Michelangelo once said of Raphael, "Everything he knows about art, he got from me."

Raphael's Growing Popularity

In 1504, when Raphael was twenty-one, he moved to Florence where Michelangelo and Leonardo were already living. There, he studied the

A medieval Madonna by Giovanni Cimabue

techniques of the older artists and learned to use them in his own paintings.

Remember, in those days artists supported themselves by getting commissions from patrons. The wealthy people of Florence were eager to own beautiful paintings. By the time Raphael arrived, both Leonardo and Michelangelo were not painting as much. As he aged, Leonardo grew more interested in math and science and was reluctant to paint at all. Michelangelo's energies were consumed by big projects assigned to him by the pope. So, young Raphael had many people ready to pay him to paint.

While in Florence, Raphael created at least seventeen paintings of the Madonna and the Holy Family for various individuals. Let's take a look at one of Raphael's Madonnas and compare it to a Madonna painted earlier, during the Middle Ages. This will help you see how people's view of the world changed in the Renaissance.

In the pictures here, you can see how the medieval Madonna looks stiff and artificial. But the painting wasn't intended to be lifelike—its main purpose was to express religious devotion.

But look at Raphael's painting. He presents very natural, human figures. You can see the love between a mother and a child. While Raphael's painting is religious, it is also warm, vital, and human.

There are special names for two familiar kinds of religious paintings. A *Madonna* is a picture of Mary, the mother of Jesus. A *Holy Family* is a picture of Jesus and his parents, Mary and Joseph.

Raphael's *Small Cowper Madonna*

The School of Athens

Raphael in Rome

In 1508 Raphael was called to Rome by Pope Julius II, the "Warrior Pope." While Michelangelo was painting the ceiling of the Sistine Chapel, Raphael was put in charge of painting a series of rooms in the Vatican.

In *The School of Athens*, when Raphael painted this figure of Plato, he used the face of Leonardo da Vinci.

In one room he painted a fresco that has become very famous. It is called The School of Athens. The composition of the painting shows how Raphael was a great master of perspective, while the subject matter shows how much the Renaissance admired the ancient Greeks. Raphael painted many scholars and philosophers—some are reading, some are discussing big ideas. In the center of the painting, Raphael placed the great philosophers, Plato and Aristotle.

After Julius died, Raphael became a special favorite of Pope Leo X. Leo put Raphael in charge of the work on St. Peter's Basilica. In addition, Raphael directed the efforts to dig up and study ancient buildings and statues in Rome.

Raphael had a productive life, but a short one. The artist died on his thirty-seventh birthday. Part of the epitaph on his tomb in Rome reads, "While he lived he made Mother Nature fear to be vanquished by him."

Epitaph: Words written on a tombstone in memory of the person buried there.

Most art historians agree that this face from *The School of Athens* is a picture of Raphael himself.

Part II The Renaissance Beyond Italy: Painters, Composers, and Writers

Introduction
Not Just in Italy

Until now, we have only talked about the Italian Renaissance. Did a "rebirth" occur in other parts of Europe, also?

Yes. Scholars and artists in other countries were also enjoying a rebirth of learning. Sometimes these scholars and artists visited the city-states of Italy, especially Florence, and brought ideas and artwork home to their own countries. These countries included Germany and the region that used to be called Flanders, which is now part of the Netherlands and Belgium. (You can find the Netherlands on the map facing page 1.)

You're about to meet three painters: one was from Germany, and two were Flemish, which means they were from Flanders. Because these painters lived in countries north of Italy, people often say that they are part of "The Northern Renaissance."

After you read about these painters, you're going to meet some composers and learn about how music changed during the Renaissance. And then you'll get to know two great writers, one from Spain and one from England.

Here's looking at you, kid. But do you know who's doing the looking?

Chapter 10

Three from the Northern Renaissance

The Master of Detail

The "King of the Painters"—that's what his countrymen called Jan van Eyck [van IKE]. Van Eyck was born in about 1390 and lived in Flanders. He is a very early figure in the Northern Renaissance. He painted at about the same time that Brunelleschi was working as an architect in Italy.

Van Eyck developed new kinds of oil paint that gave his pictures a sharp and brilliant look. He discovered new ways to show light and texture in his paintings. He could realistically portray the tiniest details in a picture. Look at the picture of *Giovanni Arnolfini and His Wife*, a portrait that Van Eyck painted for an Italian businessman living in Flanders. Notice how Van Eyck has rendered the texture of the groom's robes and the bride's dress, as well as the light pouring through the open window.

Van Eyck painted *Giovanni Arnolfini and His Wife* in 1434. (The painting is also known as *The Arnolfini Wedding*.)

Are the bride and groom the only people in the room? No, but you have to look closely to find out. The mirror on the back wall shows two other persons in the room—probably Van Eyck himself and another man who came to witness the marriage.

Some of the details in the picture of the Arnolfini wedding had special meanings for viewers in Van Eyck's time. For example, the little dog stands for faithfulness and love. The fruit on the window sill means that the couple hope their marriage will be "fruitful," in other words, that they will have children.

Dürer: Self-Portrait of the Artist

Albrecht Dürer [DUR-er] was born in 1471 in Germany. (He was just a little older than Michelangelo, who was born in 1475.) He made two trips to Italy in order to learn as much as he could from the great masters.

While visiting Italy, Dürer noticed that the citizens there honored sculptors and painters. But in Germany, people still thought of artists as craftsmen or laborers hired to do a job—which is the way artists had been viewed throughout Europe during the Middle Ages. While in Italy, said Dürer, "I am a gentleman, [but] at home I am a parasite."

Dürer drew this self-portrait when he was only thirteen years old.

Dürer wanted to insist on his dignity and pride as an artist. These qualities come through in his many self-portraits. The very fact that Dürer painted so many self-portraits shows his Renaissance attitude. It shows his belief in the importance of the individual, especially one particular individual, himself!

One of the earliest works we have by Dürer is a drawing he made of himself when he was only thirteen. In the *Self-Portrait* he painted in 1498, Dürer shows himself as a handsome young man with a taste for fine clothes. In the famous *Self-Portrait* painted in 1500,

***Self-Portrait*, 1498**

Dürer looks directly at us with bold, confident eyes.

Dürer was not only a great painter, he was also a master of the art of making prints with woodcuts or engravings. As a young apprentice he learned how to make woodcuts by carving pictures in blocks of wood, as well as engravings by using a sharp tool to press an image on a metal plate. He would spread ink on the carved wood or the metal plate, then print the image on paper. Dürer's woodcuts and engravings made him famous, partly because they

***Self-Portrait*, 1500**

FROM THE MUSEUM OF FINE ARTS, BOSTON

***Knight, Death and the Devil,* an engraving done by Albrecht Dürer in 1513**

could be quickly and easily reproduced, so many people could see them.

Pieter Bruegel: Pictures of Everyday Life

Pieter Bruegel [BROY-gul] was born in the city of Antwerp, which is in the country we now call Belgium. Like Venice and Florence in Italy, Antwerp was a busy trading city with many banks and businesses—which meant there were many wealthy people ready to buy works of art. Most of these people wanted paintings in the style of the great Italian masters such as Michelangelo and Raphael. So Bruegel traveled to Italy to see what he could learn.

When it came to painting however, Bruegel went his own way. You won't find heroic-looking, muscular figures such as Michelangelo painted on the ceiling of the Sistine Chapel. You won't find many scenes from classical mythology in Bruegel. His paintings are

Landscape with the Fall of Icarus

very different from anything like Botticelli's *Birth of Venus*.

Let's look at one of the few paintings in which Bruegel did choose to use a classical myth. In *Landscape with the Fall of Icarus*, it's as though Bruegel were saying, "All these paintings about gods and goddesses and heroes! What's all the fuss about these myths? I'll give you a painting about a myth, but in my own way."

Bruegel's way was to make the myth only a small part of the painting. He chose the Greek myth of Daedalus [DED-ah-lus], the master inventor, and his son Icarus [IK-er-us]. For King Minos, Daedalus designed a giant maze called the Labyrinth, from which no one could escape. Later, when the king grew angry at Daedalus, he locked him in the Labyrinth along with Icarus. But Daedalus soon came up with a plan to escape. Little by little, he gathered many feathers, then fastened them together with wax to make wings like those of a bird. He and his son used the wings to fly out of the Labyrinth. But in his excitement Icarus ignored his father's warnings not to fly too high. Up and up he flew until the sun began to melt the wax. The feathers fell from his wings, and down plunged Icarus into the sea.

Bruegel's painting shows the fall of Icarus, though at first glance you might not even notice it. Look at the bottom right corner of the painting. Do you see two legs sticking out of the water near the ship? That's Icarus falling into the water—and that's all of the myth Bruegel chose to show. Bruegel draws our attention away from the myth and makes us look at everyday life, at the farmer plowing and the shepherd with his flock.

Bruegel is best known for his pictures of everyday people. For example, look at *Peasant Wedding* (also known as *The Wedding Feast*), painted in the late 1560s. Bruegel shows the peasants as he saw them. He doesn't try to "prettify" the scene. This is not a fancy feast. The simple food is being carried on rough boards. In the foreground, you can see a child licking her fingers, making sure she gets every last bit out of the bowl. In the middle left, the piper is looking hungrily at the food passing by. He's probably hoping there will be some food left for him after he finishes playing!

Peasant Wedding

Bruegel's sons, grandsons, and even great-grandsons became artists. But none equaled or surpassed his great works.

Chapter 11

Masses, Dances, and Love Songs: Music in the Renaissance

Music Changes During a Time of Change

The Renaissance was a time of discovery, exploration, and invention—in other words, a time of great change. You've seen how the arts of painting and sculpture changed during the Renaissance. What about music?

Music changed too. To appreciate how it changed, you need to know a little about what music was like *before* the Renaissance.

During the Middle Ages, music was most important in churches and monasteries, where priests, monks, and nuns sang praises to God. Generally they sang religious words in Latin, and they all sang the same melody. To our modern-day ears, this kind of singing, called plainsong or plainchant (or "chant" for short) can sound mysterious but also soothing.

During the Renaissance, as more and more people became interested in science, philosophy, paintings, and sculptures, they also became more interested in music. These people were not just monks or scholars. They were the merchants and their families in the cities, as well as the nobility, the people of the upper classes, in courts throughout Europe. They wanted to enjoy music not just in church but also in their homes. These people began to think that for a person to be well-rounded and well-educated, it was important to know how to read music and be able to sing.

In the monasteries, monks developed the first system for writing down music. Most of the music that was sung and played outside the churches was not written down.

Some of these people began to experiment with different ways of singing. They discovered that they could get a beautiful sound when two or three people sang at the same time, but instead of all singing the same notes (as monks did when they sang chants), each singer would sing different notes. It's something like what happens when you and your friends sing a round, such as "Frère Jacques" or "Row, Row, Row Your Boat."

When different singers sing different notes at the same time, and the notes come together to produce a pleasing sound, then the singers are singing in *harmony*. In the kind of singing that developed during the Renaissance, each voice sang its own melody and sounded pretty all by itself, but sounded even more beautiful when combined with other voices. This combining of voices singing different melodies in harmony is called *polyphony* [puh-LIF-uh-nee], a word which comes from Greek words meaning "many voices." The invention of polyphony was probably the single most important change to happen to music during the Renaissance.

Also during the Renaissance, many musicians started writing their own music. Some became famous composers who traveled from court to court and city to city. This was something new. Back in the Middle Ages, composers often remained unknown. We know of only a few medieval composers, but there are many famous Renaissance composers. Most of them wrote both *sacred* music (music for the church) and *secular* music (music for everyday life).

Sacred Music: Masses

One of the most important forms of sacred music was the *Mass*. The Mass is the Catholic church service that celebrates Christ's Last Supper and sacrifice on the cross. When the words to the Mass, which were in Latin, were sung by a small group or large choir, they could sound very beautiful.

Composers sometime wrote Masses in a style called *a cappella*, which means "in the style of the chapel." *A cappella* works were written to be sung by voices alone, without instruments, so that the words could be clearly heard and understood. Today we still use the term *a cappella* to describe any kind of choral music sung without instruments playing along.

Josquin Desprez [ZHOS-kan day-PRAY], who was born in about 1450, wrote nearly twenty Masses. He was widely admired as one of the greatest composers of the Renaissance. He came from what is now the Netherlands, but mostly worked as a singer and composer for princes and the pope in Italy.

Secular Music: Songs and Dances

Josquin Desprez didn't just write sacred music; he also wrote secular music, music that people would enjoy outside of church. Secular music during the Renaissance included songs that had to do with love or told amusing stories. One song Josquin wrote is called *Faulte d'argent*, which, if you loosely translate the French title, means, "I need money!"

Many popular Renaissance songs were written for four or five voices and sung in polyphony. These songs were called *madrigals*. Like popular songs today, many madrigals were about—what would you guess?—yes, love, of course. The Italian composer known as Palestrina [pah-lace-TREE-nah] wrote four books of madrigals. But Palestrina was mainly a composer of sacred music. He wrote more than ninety Masses! He once said, "I blush and grieve" about writing the madrigals.

Besides singing, people also liked to dance. At the courts of princes and kings, dances were a favorite occasion. Renaissance composers wrote a lot of dance music. Dance music was written for instruments, not voices.

Often, dances were played in pairs, one slow and one fast. For example, first the musicians might play a *pavane* [puh-VAHN], a slow and formal dance that included many bows and curtsies. Then they would play a *galliard* [GAL-yerd], a lively dance in which the men would hop into the air!

New Instruments and Lute Songs

Many new instruments were invented during the Renaissance. The recorder, which you may know, is a Renaissance instrument that's still popular today. It's made of wood and sounds like a flute.

A recorder

One of the most popular instruments in the Renaissance was the lute, which was something like a modern-day guitar. The lute was not a new instrument: it came from an Arab instrument called the *'ud*. The lute sounds sweet and gentle, perfect for love songs.

The greatest composer of lute music was probably John Dowland, who was born in England in 1563. One of his lute tunes, called *Lachrimae*, became the most popular tune of his time, all over Europe—and this was before radio and MTV!

Dowland also wrote many short songs for one singer accompanied by a lute. Many of these lute songs were sad and melancholy, with titles like "Sorrow Stay" and "In Darkness Let Me Dwell." Even Dowland's big number-one hit, *Lachrimae*, was a sad-sounding melody—which makes sense, because *lachrimae* is the Latin word for "tears."

Greensleeves

Here is part of a favorite song from the Renaissance. We don't know who composed it (in other words, the composer is anonymous). But people today still love to sing "Greensleeves." This song has the same melody as a popular Christmas carol, "What Child Is This?"

Alas, my love, you do me wrong
To cast me off discourteously,
For I have loved you so long
Delighting in your company.

Greensleeves was all my joy,
Greensleeves was my delight,
Greensleeves was my heart of gold,
And who but my lady Greensleeves.

A lute

No matter what you read about the music of the Renaissance, to really appreciate it you need to hear it. Your local library may have recordings that you can listen to. Also, see the recordings listed under "Resources" on page 100 in this book.

Chapter 12

Of Windmills and Star-Cross'd Lovers: Two Great Renaissance Writers

Are You "Quixotic"?

Do you know someone who is quixotic [quick-SOT-ik]? A quixotic person is a dreamer, someone who always has his or her head in the clouds, full of lofty and noble thoughts, but not very practical.

"Quixotic" is a strange word, isn't it? It comes from the name of the hero of a book called *Don Quixote* [key-HO-tay], by the Spanish writer Miguel de Cervantes [me-GHEL day ser-VAN-tees].

When Cervantes published the first part of *Don Quixote* in 1605, it was a big hit. People loved the book. And people still do. It has been translated from Spanish into more than a hundred languages, including English, Japanese, Arabic, Hebrew, and even Tibetan! Only the Bible has been translated more often. Composers have written music and operas about Don Quixote. Artists have painted pictures and carved statues of him. In our own time, there has even been a Broadway play based on *Don Quixote*, which was made into a movie (called *Man of La Mancha*).

Before you read more about this great book, let's get to know the author.

Bad Luck Trails a Good Man

Cervantes

Miguel de Cervantes was born in Spain in 1547. As a young man, Cervantes published some poems. But he did not set out to be a writer. Instead he became a soldier. He joined a Spanish regiment stationed in Naples.

In 1571, Cervantes fought against the Turks in a naval battle. About forty men on the ship, including the captain, were killed. Two bullets hit Cervantes in the chest, and a third permanently maimed his left hand. But Cervantes survived and made a slow recovery.

After six years as a soldier, Cervantes headed back to Spain. With him, he carried letters that gloriously described his military service. He thought these papers might help him find a good job when he got back home.

Instead, the letters became a curse to him.

This is what happened. Just off the coast of France, Cervantes's ship was attacked by pirates. When the pirates read the letters, they assumed they had captured an important and wealthy gentleman. So they took Cervantes to Algeria, where they threw him into prison and held him for a high ransom. He tried to escape many times, but never made it. Finally, after five years, Cervantes's family was able to scrape up the necessary money to set him free.

Back in Jail

When a soldier with a distinguished war record returned from battle, he could usually get a good job with a nobleman. But Cervantes received no such reward. So there he was, thirty-three years old and out of work. What to do? Well, why not try writing again?

And boy, did he write! Cervantes churned out dozens and dozens of poems and plays. Although people liked his work, he still didn't make much money. To put bread on the table, he took a job with the government.

In one of his government jobs, Cervantes got into trouble again. He was working as a tax collector—a job that's not likely to help anyone win a popularity contest. Anyway, as far as we can tell from the available evidence, here's how Cervantes got in trouble. Once, when he had collected a lot of tax money, Cervantes felt anxious about carrying it as he traveled along the roads. So he left the money with an innkeeper he thought he could trust. When he returned to get the money, the innkeeper had run off with it! The government held Cervantes responsible for the stolen money. Since he couldn't repay it all, he was thrown in jail.

Some people believe that while Cervantes was in jail, he came up with the idea for *Don Quixote*, and perhaps even wrote some of the book behind bars. If that's true, then the time in jail was well spent. When Cervantes published *The History of Don Quixote de la Mancha* in 1605, the book became an instant success. It made Cervantes famous, but not rich. Even though lots of people bought the book, many of the books were "pirated" copies—in other words, people printed and sold the book but never paid Cervantes a single cent. (Now we have laws, called copyright laws, to protect authors from this kind of thing.)

Near the end of his life, Cervantes did find a patron whose support allowed him to concentrate on his writing. He wrote a second part to *Don Quixote* and more short stories. He completed a novel just four days before he died in Madrid in 1616.

Don Quixote and Sancho Panza

What's So Great About *Don Quixote*?

Don Quixote was written about 400 years ago. Why has it remained so popular?

For one thing, much of the book is very funny. There's a story that once the king of Spain was looking out a window when he saw a man who, while reading a book, kept slapping his head and roaring with laughter. "I'll bet," said the king, "that he's reading *Don Quixote*."

Cervantes wrote *Don Quixote* to make fun of a certain kind of book, the romances of chivalry. These romances, which were very popular in Cervantes's time, told stories of brave knights in shining armor who set out to rescue damsels in distress. They were full of fantastic adventures, powerful magicians, fierce dragons, and brave deeds. Some of these romances were entertaining fantasies. But many were just plain ridiculous.

Chivalry is a code of conduct, a way to behave. In medieval times, knights were supposed to follow the code of chivalry, which told them to be brave, loyal, honorable, and religious, and to use their strength to protect the weak.

You can almost hear the wheels turning in Cervantes's mind: "I wonder what would happen if I took a character from these unrealistic romances and put him in a realistic setting—if I put him in Spain, right here, in my own time. Hmm . . . ."

And so Cervantes created Don Quixote. ("Don" is a title of respect, like "Sir" in English.) The Don is an elderly gentleman who loves to read romances about the knights of the Middle Ages. He loves reading these books so much that he sells part of his farmland just so he can

Don Quixote thought he was attacking a giant but he was only tilting at windmills.

named Sancho Panza, to leave his wife and children and become Don Quixote's squire. (After all, as Don Quixote tells Sancho Panza, in the romances squires are always well rewarded, and some day Sancho will become the governor of his own private island!)

So Don Quixote and Sancho Panza set off in search of adventures. When Don Quixote comes across a country inn, he believes it's a splendid castle. When he sees windmills, he thinks they are giants with many arms, and he rides to attack them. He is painfully reminded of reality when a windmill's whirling sail knocks him to the ground. Sancho Panza tries to make Don Quixote see things as they are: "Oh, Sir," Sancho cries, "didn't I tell you they were just windmills?" But Don Quixote replies, "I believe some evil enchanter turned those giants into windmills to rob me of a glorious victory. But I will triumph over him in the end!"

buy more of them. In fact, he reads so many romances that he loses touch with reality. He begins to believe the romances are true—that all the enchantments and battles and rescues really happened. Soon, he doesn't just want to read about knights anymore—instead, he decides to become one. His goal is to wander the world in search of adventures, to gain fame and honor by his daring deeds.

So Don Quixote straps on some rusty armor and hoists himself onto his ancient, limping horse. Then the old man convinces a neighbor, a laborer

A man who attacks windmills may seem foolish, and Don Quixote does many foolish things. But the more you get to know Don Quixote, the more you begin to see that he is, at heart, noble and generous—sometimes a lot more noble and generous than the world around him. Many people who read *Don Quixote* find that while they laugh at the knight, they can't help admiring the way he pursues his dream, no matter what the obstacles.

Shakespeare

Shakespeare: "All the World's a Stage"

Have you ever heard any of these expressions?

- *tongue-tied*
- *as quiet as a lamb*
- *seen better days*
- *dead as a doornail*
- *eaten out of house and home*

Have you ever come across any of these famous lines?

- *All's well that ends well.*
- *A horse! A horse! My kingdom for a horse!*
- *If music be the food of love, play on.*
- *Sweets to the sweet.*
- *O Romeo, Romeo! Wherefore art thou Romeo?*
- *Something is rotten in the state of Denmark.*
- *To be, or not to be: that is the question.*
- *Friends, Romans, countrymen, lend me your ears.*
- *All the world's a stage, and all the men and women merely players.*

Those phrases and lines come from the pen of the man most people consider the greatest playwright of all time, William Shakespeare. Along with the Bible, the works of Shakespeare have had a greater influence on English language and literature than anything by any other writers.

Shakespeare wrote many poems, but he is best known for writing plays. The plays are still performed and loved today. Some have been made into popular movies, such as *Much Ado About Nothing*, *Hamlet*, and *Romeo and Juliet*. Students across the country regularly read Shakespeare's plays, especially *A Midsummer Night's Dream*, *Romeo and Juliet*, *Julius Caesar*, *Macbeth*, and *Hamlet*. If you haven't read one of those plays yet, you probably will soon!

At a theater in Renaissance times, players perform a scene from Shakespeare's comedy *A Midsummer Night's Dream*.

Romeo and Juliet is still popular today. There are several movie versions of *Romeo and Juliet*, including this 1998 movie version starring Leonardo DiCaprio as Romeo and Claire Danes as Juliet.

Romeo and Juliet tells the tragic tale of how "a pair of star-cross'd lovers take their life." "Star-cross'd" means unlucky, as though the stars are against them. (According to popular belief in horoscopes and astrology, the stars influence human destiny.) Romeo and Juliet are unlucky because their families are fierce rivals, engaged in a bloody feud against each other. A modern-day Broadway musical, *West Side Story*, takes the basic story behind *Romeo and Juliet* and updates it, turning the feuding families into rival gangs.

The Young Bard of Avon

You might hear Shakespeare called the "Bard of Avon." *Bard* is another word for a poet. The poet we're interested in, Shakespeare, was born in England, in Stratford-upon-Avon, in 1564.

He was the third of eight children. His father worked as a leather merchant and glove maker. During Shakespeare's early years, his father served as bailiff (something like a mayor) of their town and the family seemed pretty well-off.

In Shakespeare's time, boys attended school from 6 a.m. to 5 p.m., with a two-hour break in the middle of the day. Girls stayed home. Young Will probably spent long hours learning Latin, Greek, the Bible, and English history. It seems he didn't enjoy school much: in one of his plays, he described "the whining schoolboy, with his satchel…creeping like snail unwillingly to school."

By the time Shakespeare reached college age, his father had become so poor that he owed money, couldn't pay taxes, and didn't show his face in public for fear of being thrown in jail. It's likely that the Shakespeare family didn't have enough money to pay for a college education for William.

What did William do when he finished his schooling? Some historians think he probably helped his father make gloves. Others believe he may have worked for a schoolmaster or lawyer. Another account says he may have been a butcher's apprentice. No one knows for sure.

The Lost Years

In fact, there's a lot about Shakespeare's life we don't know. No one even knows for sure the exact date of Shakespeare's birthday.

When Shakespeare was born, no one knew he was going to become the greatest playwright of all time, so of course no one stood by with a notebook keeping track of all the details of his life. Most of the information we have about Shakespeare comes from the town's official records of baptisms, marriages, and deaths. We also know a little from what his friends wrote about him. But you can't always count on those sources for accuracy.

8:00 a.m., William eats mashed apple, 8:18 a.m., William burps, 8:45 a.m., William plays with toys...

If we had only known that Shakespeare would grow up to be so famous....

Over the years, scholars have closely examined the available documents, as well as Shakespeare's own writings, to put together a picture of the playwright's life. Sometimes parts of the picture are missing, and then scholars have to use whatever evidence they have to make an informed guess.

We *do* know that eighteen-year-old William married twenty-six-year-old Anne Hathaway in 1582. Over the next few years, Anne gave birth to their daughter Susanna, followed by twins, a daughter named Judith and a son named Hamnet.

After the twins were born, Shakespeare did not linger very long in Stratford-upon-Avon. We're not certain why he left. Nor does anyone know what Shakespeare did during what are called "The Lost Years" from 1582 to 1592.

We do know that by 1592 Shakespeare had arrived in London and was establishing a reputation as a playwright, actor, and poet. Some of his more highly educated competitors said his plays were "vulgar." One critic called Shakespeare an "upstart crow." But the people loved his work, and the royalty also enjoyed them. His acting company frequently performed in the court of Queen Elizabeth and later for King James.

Shakespeare dedicated two sets of poems to the Earl of Southampton. In gratitude, the earl gave Shakespeare lots of money. Shakespeare invested the money in his acting company, the Chamberlain's Men (later called The King's Men), and in the theaters where they performed. Every time the actors performed, Shakespeare, as co-owner, could take a percentage of the profits.

Acting troupes were sponsored by wealthy patrons and were known by that patron's name or position. For example, groups were called the Lord Admiral's Men, the Earl of Leicester's Men, or the Chamberlain's Men.

The Globe Theater

Many of Shakespeare's plays were performed in the Globe Theater, which was built in 1599 on the south bank of the Thames [temz] River in London. The Globe was a wooden, circular building with an open courtyard in the middle. The theater could hold up to 2,500 people. People with little money could pay a penny to stand in the yard and watch the play; they were called the groundlings. Richer people could buy seats in the galleries, which were along three sides of the theater and were covered by a roof to protect the audience from the sun or a sudden rain. Performances were given only in daylight and only in good weather.

A performance at the Globe was different from most theaters today. Audiences could be rude and noisy. It was common for viewers to shout comments and throw objects on stage. There were no curtains on stage and hardly any scenery. For example, a forest might be indicated by a sign simply stating "The Woods." Although the scenery was simple, costumes were often quite fancy.

Did you know that in Shakespeare's time, only men acted on stage? No women were allowed to be actors! The women's parts were played by young boys who still had high voices and no beards.

In 1613, a cannon fired as part of a performance of *Henry VIII* set fire to a thatched roof, and the theater burned to the ground. But if you visit London today, you can still see a Shakespeare play at the Globe—that is, at the *new* Globe Theater.

You can visit the new Globe Theater in London today.

In the 1990s the theater was rebuilt very near its original location. Scholars and architects worked together closely to make the new Globe as much like the original as possible. The outer walls of the theater are covered with a mixture of plaster and goat hair, just what builders would have used in Shakespeare's time. Like the original theater, the new Globe has a thatched roof made of straw, but the straw used today has been coated with a special liquid to make it fireproof.

And so, as the Bard himself said, "All's well that ends well."

When Shakespeare wrote his plays, England was ruled by Queen Elizabeth I. She was a powerful and intelligent leader, and very popular with the English people. The arts thrived during the reign of Elizabeth. She filled her court with poets, playwrights, and musicians.

Part III The Reformation, *or* Watch Out for the Papal Bull

Introduction
From Artists to Priests and Popes

You're about to leave behind one historical period, the Renaissance, and examine another, the Reformation. The Reformation began in the early 1500s, during the later years of the Renaissance. When you learned about the Renaissance, you read a lot about artists and writers and inventors. But as you learn about the Reformation, you will be reading mostly about priests and monks and popes. That's because the Reformation was a time of great changes in the church and society.

To get started, we're going to go backward in time, a little before the Reformation, and meet a man named Gutenberg [GOOT-en-burg] who made an invention that changed the world. Then you'll find out about Martin Luther, a monk whose ideas started a revolution in religious thinking in Europe. Finally, you will learn about Galileo, a scientist whose life was greatly affected by the religious changes of his time.

Let's begin with Mr. Gutenberg.

It's not a weather map. What is it? You'll find out soon.

Chapter 13

Like Books? Thank Gutenberg!

Did You Say "Gooseflesh"?

Did you know that a man named "John Gooseflesh" changed the world? He really did. Forever. Johann Gensfleisch—which in English is "John Gooseflesh"—was born in Germany around 1395. You have to wonder if young Johnny Gooseflesh put up with a lot of teasing as a child.

In any case, Johann Gensfleisch decided that he would go by his mother's family name: Gutenberg. Now, let's find out why people today remember the name of Gutenberg, and how he changed the world.

Gutenberg and the Printing Press

The book you are reading is a *printed* book. There are thousands of copies of this same book, all quickly printed on machines.

Back in the Middle Ages, there were no printed books. There were books, but they were rare and expensive, because each book had to be copied out by hand, one at a time. Most of the copying was done by monks who worked patiently in their monasteries. Only the church and the wealthiest people could afford to own books. Very few people knew how to read because, after all, what was there to read?

But all this changed around 1440, when Johann Gutenberg invented a new way to make books—not by copying them one at a time by hand, but by printing many copies at once.

This picture shows a small part of an illuminated manuscript from the Middle Ages. *Illuminated* means the page is decorated with designs and illustrations.

Gutenberg figured out a way to pour melted metal into molds in the shapes of the letters of the alphabet. He arranged these metal letters into words, which

Gutenberg and his colleagues inspect the results of his printing press.

were tightly packed in a rectangular frame. Because you could reuse these metal letters and move them around to make new words, this method was called *movable type*.

Gutenberg wasn't the first to use movable type. Hundreds of years before Gutenberg, the Chinese and Koreans had used a form of movable type. Gutenberg, however, invented a machine that greatly improved the process of printing with movable type.

Gutenberg bought a wine press, a machine used to squeeze the juice out of grapes. He turned the machine into a printing press. This screw-and-lever press could push the movable type, with ink smeared on it, onto a sheet of paper. Gutenberg's printing press could print up to 300 pages a day.

A few copies of the Gutenberg Bible still exist, but they are rare and very valuable. How valuable? In 1987, a copy of the Gutenberg Bible was sold at an auction for more than five million dollars!

Sometime around 1450, Gutenberg printed his first book, the Bible. As far as we know, the Gutenberg Bible was the first book printed with movable metal type.

The Power Unleashed by the Printed Word

Soon printing presses were churning out books in many of the major cities of Europe, including Rome, Venice, Paris, and Constantinople.

By the year 1500—only about fifty years after Gutenberg's first printed book—over 40,000 books were printed in Europe. In the next century, between 1500 and 1600, over *200 million* books were printed!

At first, most of the books were printed in Latin, a language read only by philosophers, monks and priests, and some noblemen. But as time went on,

How Gutenberg's Press Worked

1. The printer set the metal type into the words and sentences that belonged on the page.
2. After the printer arranged the page properly, he clamped it with a wooden frame and rolled ink over the type.
3. Then he placed the page of type on the printing press and laid paper on top of it.
4. Next, by turning a large screw, he lowered the press onto the paper. This caused the page to be printed on the sheet.

books were published in languages that many more people could read: French, English, Italian, Spanish, and German.

Today, you can walk into a library or bookstore and choose from thousands of books. So you have to use your imagination to really appreciate just how big— I mean, absolutely *huge*— a change occurred after Gutenberg and the printing press.

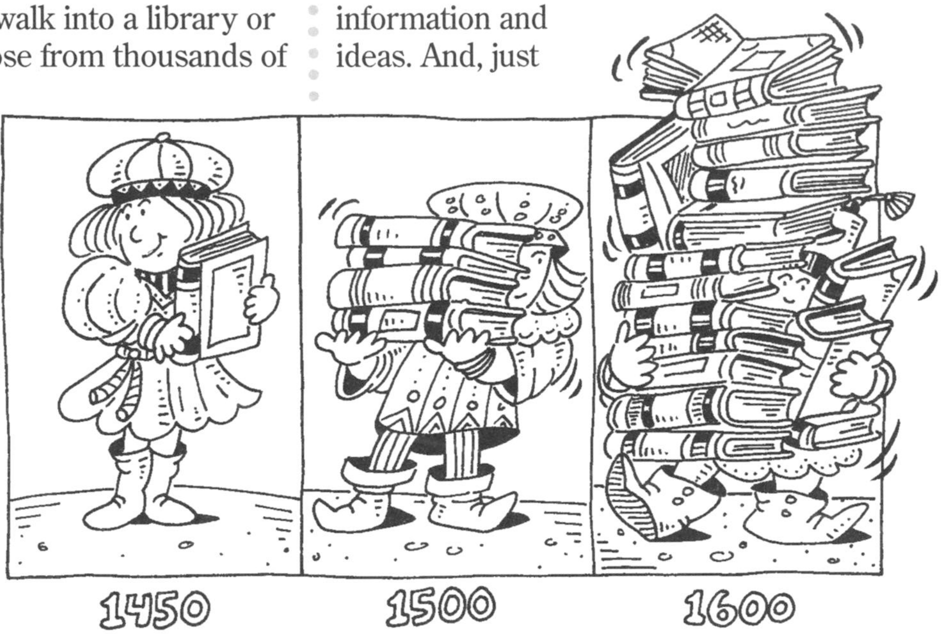

Let me repeat: Before Gutenberg, there were only a few books, which were mostly in Latin, and stuck away in monasteries. Very few people in their lifetimes would ever hold, let alone read, a book. But after Gutenberg, there were plenty of books, written in languages that people could understand. After Gutenberg, people could read about history and geography and religion. They could enjoy stories and poems. Books opened the door to a whole new world of learning and ideas.

But some people didn't like this. Some government officials worried: What if this printing press is used to spread ideas that would weaken our power over the people? Some church leaders thought: What if this printing press is used to publish ideas that contradict our beliefs?

But, as the old saying goes, "Too late to close the gate, the horse is out of the barn!" No one could stop the printing presses. No one could stop the flow of information and ideas. And, just as some church leaders feared, this meant big changes ahead.

Chapter 14

Martin Luther and the Reformation

The Powerful Catholic Church

Today, people who are Christians may belong to one of many different kinds of churches. Some may go to a Catholic church. Others may go to a Methodist, Baptist, or Presbyterian church.

Back in the Middle Ages, however, if you were a Christian living in Western Europe, then you were part of the Roman Catholic Church. During the Middle Ages, the church became very powerful throughout Europe. As the church grew more powerful, so did its leaders—the priests, bishops, and cardinals, as well as the head of the church, the pope.

Eventually, the popes began to think that they should be in charge of not just the church but of whole countries. Over time, the church grew wealthy. It owned land, chose rulers, and decided what was taught in schools. Christians were expected to obey the church's rules, believe its teachings, and give money to support it.

The pope commanded the church's army and was in charge of the church's wealth. When a pope died, then the cardinals and bishops—the highest leaders in the church (except, of course, for the pope himself)—chose a person to replace him. As you learned when you read about the popes during the Renaissance, some popes were better than others.

Not everyone in the church was happy with the way the church was growing and changing. During the Renaissance, as scholars studied classical civilizations and history, they learned about the early history of the church. Many devoted monks and priests worried that the church was losing touch with the old ways. They feared that powerful and wealthy church leaders were not spiritual enough. Some people said that some of the practices of the church were wrong and needed to be fixed. They wanted to *reform* the church—which means they wanted to change it, to fix what was wrong.

This woodblock print from the Renaissance shows a bishop.

In the early 1500s—about the time of the later years of the Renaissance—this movement to reform the church was sparked by the actions of a man named Martin Luther. Luther's actions and ideas were a major part of the great changes in the church and society which we call the *Reformation*.

A Lightning Flash

Martin Luther was one of eight children born to a poor German peasant family. Luther's father, a miner, worked hard to make sure his son could attend a university. Luther was an excellent student. When he was only twenty-one, he began to study law at the university. But he did not complete even a single semester.

What happened? As Martin Luther later told the story, he had a number of close brushes with death, which changed his attitudes about life. One such incident happened on a stormy summer night. As Luther walked home alone, thunder crashed around him, and lightning blazed across the sky. Suddenly a bolt of lightning struck, knocking Luther to the ground.

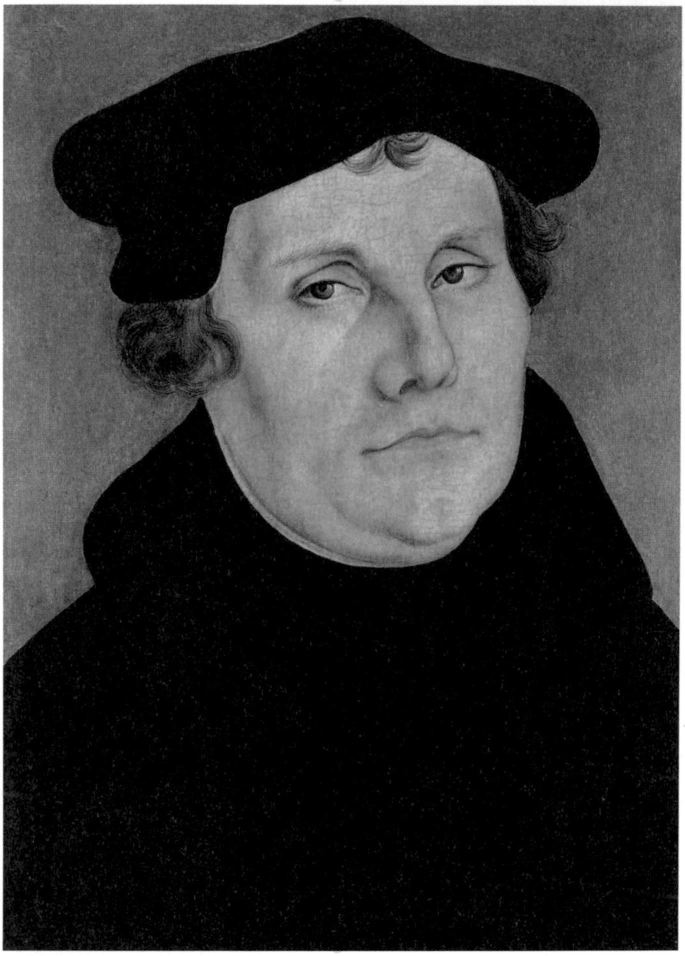

A portrait of Martin Luther, painted by Lucas Cranach

The storm raged around him. Terrified, Luther screamed, "St. Anne, help me!" He vowed that if he survived the storm, he would give his life to God and become a monk.

Luther did survive. True to his promise, but much to his father's dismay, he quit studying law and entered a monastery.

Faith and Forgiveness

Like many Christians of his time, Luther believed that the only way to escape hellfire was to do good works, give to the poor, confess his sins, and live faithfully according to the ways of the church. But the more Luther thought about it, the more convinced he became that he could never be good enough to go to heaven. The somber monk saw God as a stern judge who would most certainly condemn him.

Luther studied the Bible for hours on end. As he read and thought about the words in the Bible, his thinking began to change. He came to some revolutionary conclusions. He decided that God was not so much a stern judge as a loving father. He also concluded that doing good works and observing church law would not get you to heaven. Instead, Luther said, a person could only be saved by his or her faith in God.

Luther also said that people didn't need priests to obtain forgiveness from God for their sins. Instead, said Luther, if people confessed their sins, were sorry, and had faith, then God would forgive them. This was an important point, and it threatened the church, because Luther was questioning just how much people really needed priests.

Luther's Ninety-five Theses

Martin Luther became a professor at the University of Wittenberg. Many students and professors listened to his new ideas.

For a moment, let's leave Martin Luther teaching in Wittenberg and turn our attention to what was going on at about the same time in Rome. In Rome, the youngest son of Lorenzo de' Medici had been named Pope Leo X. Leo had big plans for his reign as pope. He intended to rebuild St. Peter's Basilica. (You might recall that Michelangelo and Raphael worked as architects on the design of St. Peter's.) The project would cost millions.

One way Pope Leo raised money was by selling over 2,000 high-powered jobs in the church. If a person could pay a lot of money, then he could become a cardinal or bishop. The person's back-ground or character didn't matter much, as long as he had the cash. The result, as you might imagine, was more than a few incompetent and even dishonest church officials.

Leo X also raised money by sending people out to sell indulgences, which were sometimes called pardons. The church said that if people bought indulgences, their sins would be pardoned, and so they could lessen the punishment they would suffer in the afterlife. Many peasants, who did not have much money, bought indulgences, hoping to get a better chance of being saved and going to heaven.

The practice of selling indulgences infuriated Martin Luther. Luther said that only faith and God's mercy could save a person—in other words, you cannot buy your way into heaven.

Luther thought that the practice of selling indulgences was a sign of greed and corruption in the church. He decided to let other people know what he thought. In Latin—the language normally used by scholars in his time—Luther wrote his objections to the practice of selling indulgences. In all, he came up with ninety-five arguments against indulgences. On October 31, 1517, he nailed this document, called the Ninety-five Theses, to the door of the church at the University of Wittenberg.

From Luther's Ninety-five Theses

•

CHRISTIANS SHOULD BE TAUGHT THAT HE WHO GIVES TO A POOR MAN OR LENDS TO A NEEDY MAN, DOES BETTER THAN IF HE BOUGHT PARDONS.

•

BUT WHO OPPOSES THE GREED AND LICENSE OF THE PREACHERS OF PARDONS, LET HIM BE BLESSED.

•

WHY DOES NOT THE POPE, WHOSE RICHES ARE AT THIS DAY MORE AMPLE THAN THOSE OF THE WEALTHIEST OF THE WEALTHY, BUILD THE ONE BASILICA OF ST. PETER'S WITH HIS OWN MONEY, RATHER THAN WITH THAT OF POOR BELIEVERS?

Martin Luther prepares to burn the papal bull.

His Ideas Spread Like Wildfire

By nailing his Ninety-five Theses to the church door, Luther was trying to start a discussion. It was as though he were putting a notice on a bulletin board and asking people to respond to his ideas. But his ideas proved so powerful that they sparked a protest that led to huge changes across Europe.

Soon after Luther nailed his Ninety-five Theses to the church door, they were translated from Latin into German. Now many more people could read them. And many more people got the chance to read them. Can you guess why? Because of the printing press. In less than a month's time, people across Europe held copies of Luther's words in their hands.

Luther's ideas spread like wildfire. He wrote many essays in which he talked about the importance of faith and criticized the corrupt practices of the church. His writings were printed in small pamphlets, and thousands of copies were spread across Europe.

Luther's ideas appealed to the people. His attacks on the greed of the church pleased over-taxed peasants. But it was more than money that made Luther's ideas powerful. He taught that all believers were equal. He said that if any church official told a person to do something against his own conscience or forbidden by the Bible, then he should ignore the church official.

Of course this did not please the leaders of the church. Pope Leo X called Luther "a wild boar [who] has invaded [the Lord's] vineyard." Another official of the church said Luther had "a brain of brass and a nose of iron."

Look Out for the Papal Bull!

The pope was furious. He decided to strike back at Luther. In 1520, he issued a papal bull. "Papal" means anything having to do with the pope. And "bull" in this case does *not* have anything to do with a snorting barnyard animal. In this case, "bull" is the word for an official document issued by the pope.

Important orders issued by the pope were written on parchment (a goatskin or sheepskin especially prepared for writing), then sealed with a lump of lead. To make the document official, the pope pressed his signet ring into the lump of soft lead, which was called a *bulla* in Latin. And that's why the order is called a bull!

In his papal bull, the pope attacked Luther. The pope required all members of the church to burn Luther's writings and warned that anyone following Luther would be considered a heretic—a person who openly disagrees with the official beliefs of the church.

How did Luther respond? Defiantly! In December of 1520, students, professors, and the townspeople of Wittenberg gathered before a blazing bonfire. They watched as Martin Luther dropped a copy of the papal bull into the blaze. Luther said, "As thou hast wasted the Holy One of God, so may the eternal flames waste thee."

Luther had gone far beyond simply arguing with the church about indulgences. He had publicly defied the pope. He had made a break with the church. A month later, the pope made it official: he excommunicated Luther, that is, he took away Luther's membership in the church.

The Diet of Worms: *Not* a High-Protein Meal

Does the title of this chapter remind you of a playground song?

Nobody loves me,
Everybody hates me,
I'm gonna eat some worms.

Don't worry, nobody is going to eat any worms. Really.

So what's all this about a Diet of Worms? Well, Worms is a place, a city in Germany. The diet was the name of an assembly of Germans, including knights and representatives from various towns and regions.

In 1521, Martin Luther was ordered to appear before the Diet of Worms. He was told that he would not be harmed, so he went to Worms, where he hoped to have a chance to defend his ideas.

Instead, when he arrived at the meeting, church officials piled his writings in front of him. They ordered him to recant, which means to take back all that he had said. But Martin Luther refused. He said to the church officials, "Here I stand, I cannot do otherwise. God help me. Amen."

The Diet declared Luther a heretic and criminal. They gave him twenty-one days of safety. After that, anyone could legally murder Luther.

Fortunately, Luther had a powerful friend, Prince Frederick of Saxony (in northern Germany). As Luther traveled back to Wittenberg, the prince arranged for five masked horsemen to pretend to kidnap Luther. They took him to a castle and didn't tell anyone where he was. Some people believed he was dead.

Luther hid in the castle for ten months. He didn't waste time. He worked hard to translate the whole New Testament into German, so that his countrymen could easily read the Bible for themselves.

> **MARTIN LUTHER**
> **IN HIS OWN WORDS**
>
> •
>
> PEOPLE WHO DO NOT LIKE CHILDREN ARE SWINE, DUNCES, AND BLOCKHEADS, NOT WORTHY TO BE CALLED MEN AND WOMEN.
>
> •
>
> TEMPTATIONS, OF COURSE, CANNOT BE AVOIDED, BUT BECAUSE WE CANNOT PREVENT THE BIRDS FROM FLYING OVER OUR HEADS, THERE IS NO NEED THAT WE SHOULD LET THEM NEST IN OUR HAIR.
>
> •
>
> A LIE IS LIKE A SNOWBALL. THE LONGER IT IS ROLLED ON THE GROUND, THE LARGER IT BECOMES.
>
> •
>
> IF I REST, I RUST.

Why They're Called "Protestants"

Because of Martin Luther, people began to leave the Roman Catholic Church. They no longer believed they had to obey the pope. These people who *protest*ed against the practices and beliefs of the church came to be called *Protestants*. (That is why you may sometimes hear the Reformation referred to as the Protestant Reformation.)

After Luther, Christians were divided into Catholics and Protestants. In the United States today, Catholics and Protestants can be neighbors and friends. But in Luther's time, they were bitter enemies. Each side believed it was right. Wars and fighting broke out. Different groups of Protestants even fought against each other, since they did not all agree with each other about religious beliefs and practices. Some people were tortured, hanged, or burned at the stake over these issues. It's sad to say but history is full of examples of people doing horrible things to each other in the name of religion.

As for Martin Luther, unlike many of the people who opposed the Catholic church in his time, he was neither hanged nor burned at the stake. He returned to Wittenberg and kept preaching and writing for the rest of his life. Before he died in 1546, Luther wrote over 60,000 pages. Yet he once said that he would be happy if "all my books could disappear and the Scripture alone would be read."

Chapter 15

More Protestants, and the Counter Reformation

John Calvin

Not long after Martin Luther nailed his Ninety-five Theses to the church door in Wittenberg, another man took a leading role in the Reformation in Europe. He was a Frenchman named John Calvin. Officials of the Catholic church forced him to leave France in 1534. He moved around for a couple of years and eventually settled in Switzerland, in the city of Geneva. His ideas and teaching attracted many followers, and soon Geneva became the center of the Protestant movement known as Calvinism.

Calvin threw out many of the traditions of the Catholic church. He believed that if the Bible did not tell you to do something in the church service, then you shouldn't do it. Compared to a Catholic cathedral, a Calvinist church was very plain and bare. There were no stained glass windows, no statues of saints, no paintings. Everything was kept simple, almost severe.

Calvin emphasized an idea called "predestination," which is the belief that some people have already been chosen by God to be saved. Those chosen for salvation, said Calvin, would lead a strict and self-disciplined life, devoted to God.

Because of Calvin, the city of Geneva passed laws forbidding dancing, swearing, and gambling. Everyone had to attend church. In church, people had to follow strict rules against laughing or making noise.

John Calvin

Calvin also worked for better hospitals and special care for poor and handicapped people. He started a school called the Geneva Academy. When it opened it 1559, 900 students

In England, some religious groups studied Calvin's writings and agreed with him. One such group was the Puritans. They brought many of Calvin's ideas with them when they came to New England in the early 1600s and established the Massachusetts Bay Colony.

Henry VIII

enrolled. Graduates of the Academy traveled to many countries, including France, England, Scotland, and eventually America.

Meanwhile in England: Henry VIII

Martin Luther and John Calvin broke away from the Catholic church for religious reasons. At about the same time, the king of England, Henry VIII, decided to break from the Catholic church as well—but for very different reasons.

In about the year 1530, Henry VIII married Catherine of Aragon. She gave birth to a daughter, but Henry wanted a son to inherit the throne. Henry was an impatient, strong-willed man, and he wanted a son as soon as possible. Since Catherine had given birth to a daughter, then, as Henry saw it, there was only one thing to do—divorce her and get a new wife.

But the Catholic church did not allow divorce, and the pope would not make a special exception for Henry. Very well, said Henry, I will divorce her anyway. He did, and quickly married another woman.

Did Henry VIII get his son? Yes—not by his second wife, however, but by his third wife (though the unfortunate woman died in child-birth). In all, Henry VIII had six wives. It was risky to marry Henry: he divorced two of his wives, and had two executed.

The pope responded by excommunicating Henry. Very well again, said Henry, I will establish a new church—and he did, the Church of England. And who do you suppose would be the supreme head of the Church of England? Why, the king, of course. When some people refused to accept the king as the head of the church, they were, upon Henry's cold and merciless order, executed.

The Church of England is also called the Anglican Church.

The Counter Reformation: Catholics Clean House

Many Catholics—including nuns, priests, and everyday folk—wanted to reform the Catholic church without leaving the church.

Leaders of the Catholic church also began to realize that they had to take Martin Luther seriously. The Protestant Reformation was not going to fade away.

So the Catholic church decided to reform itself. In 1545, Pope Paul III brought together church leaders in a group called the Council of Trent. The Council worked for years to fix what was wrong in the church.

This movement within the Catholic church to reform itself became known as the *Counter Reformation.* (You may also hear this movement referred to as the Catholic Reformation.) The main goals of the Counter Reformation were:

• to weed out corrupt practices within the church,

• to state clearly the beliefs that all Catholics had to embrace, and

• to stop the spread of the Protestantism, by force if necessary.

Put Down That Book!

Earlier in this book you read about Gutenberg and the invention of the printing press. By the time the Council of Trent met, hundreds of thousands of books were in print. To the church leaders, this was not entirely a good thing, because some of these books did not agree with the beliefs and practices of the Catholic church.

Church leaders recognized the power of the printed word. So the Council of Trent decided to control what Catholics could read. They said all books must be reviewed before they could be published. Also, they made a list of banned publications, called the Index of Forbidden Books. If the church leaders thought a book went against the teachings of the church, then the book was banned. Books by Martin Luther and John Calvin were banned. Anyone caught reading, selling, or owning a banned book could be excommunicated.

Saint Ignatius of Loyola

Around 1540, a Spanish priest named Ignatius [ig-NAY-shus] of Loyola founded a new group within the Catholic church, called the Society of Jesus, or Jesuits.

Ignatius did not start out as a very religious man. He spent his young adult years fighting in the Spanish military. While he was battling against the French, a cannonball severely injured both of his legs. Flat on his back for months, about the only thing he could do was read. He read about the life of Christ, and his reading deeply changed his views on life. The soldier left his military life behind and set off to become a priest.

Saint Ignatius of Loyola

While studying for the priesthood in Paris, Ignatius lived in poverty and spent much time writing his ideas. He believed that a person needed to repent from sin and model his life after Jesus. With some of his colleagues, he formed the Society of Jesus.

Jesuits lived lives of poverty and religious service. Many Jesuits traveled far and wide as missionaries, spreading Catholicism around the world. Throughout the years that followed, Jesuits also became great leaders in education.

Ignatius was declared a saint by the Catholic church, so he is now called Saint Ignatius.

Chapter16

Galileo: Rebel with a Cause

The Wrangler

If you ask lots of questions in class, and they're good questions, your teacher is likely to think of you as a bright student.

Not so in Galileo's day. Born in Italy in 1564, Galileo [gal-uh-LAY-oh *or* gal-uh-LEE- oh] would grow up to become a great scientist. As a young student, he was nicknamed "the Wrangler" because he asked so many questions and argued so much with both teachers and students. He had a reputation for being rude and arrogant.

In Galileo's time, students were expected to accept knowledge handed down from the great scholars and philosophers of ancient Greece and Rome, especially Aristotle, who lived in Greece way back in the fourth century B.C. Everyone thought Aristotle and other ancient philosophers knew all there was to know about the natural world. Nothing they said could be improved upon. They were *the authorities* —you were supposed to believe them, not question them.

Aristotle

But Galileo did not hesitate to question authority, even the great Aristotle. For example, in Galileo's time people believed that if you dropped two objects of different weights, the heavier object would fall faster and hit the ground first. They believed it because Aristotle had said so. According to Aristotle, an object that weighs ten pounds should fall ten times faster than an object that weighs one pound.

But the more Galileo thought about this, the more he thought Aristotle was wrong—and he decided to prove it. At the time, he was a young man teaching mathematics at the University of Pisa [PEE-zuh]. According to a famous story, Galileo invited his students and fellow professors to watch an experiment. They gathered near the Leaning Tower of Pisa and listened as Galileo said something like this: "From the top of the tower I will drop two cannonballs, a small one and a big one. If Aristotle is right, the bigger, heavier cannonball will hit the ground first—but I think he is wrong."

Who does this young upstart think he is? How dare he question the wisdom of Aristotle?

Galileo climbed the steps to the top of the tower. Then he carefully released the two cannonballs at the same time. Down, down they fell—and struck the earth at the exact same instant.

Galileo showed that Aristotle was wrong. Even more important, Galileo discovered the law of falling bodies, which says that objects fall at the same rate, regardless of what they weigh. While Galileo did in fact make this discovery, some historians doubt whether he actually dropped the cannonballs from the Leaning Tower of Pisa. The story survives, however, because it tells us something important about Galileo. It shows how he believed you shouldn't have to accept an idea just because someone else claims it is true. He believed you have to support your ideas with evidence.

These beliefs got Galileo into big trouble with the Catholic church. But to understand how that happened, first we need to go back several centuries before Galileo's time, all the way to ancient times.

From Earth-Centered to Sun-Centered: Ptolemy and Copernicus

In school you've probably learned about the solar system. You know that the earth and the other planets orbit around the sun. But people in Galileo's time didn't know this.

Ptolemy

In Galileo's time, most people believed in the system described way back in ancient times by the Greek philosopher Aristotle and, in the second century A.D., by Ptolemy [TALL-uh-me], a Greek astronomer and mathematician who lived in Egypt.

Ptolemy supported Aristotle's view that the earth stood still at the center of the universe, while the sun, moon, and planets all revolved around the earth. He thought these heavenly bodies were located in different spheres—something like gigantic, crystal-clear bubbles—

"Mr. Galileo was correct!"

What is the force that makes things fall? It's gravity.

You can try Galileo's experiment at home. When you do the experiment, try to drop objects of similar shape, for example, an orange and a grape. If you drop an orange and a piece of paper, the experiment won't work: the orange will fall quickly but the piece of paper will float down slowly. That's because in this case something more than gravity is at work. The paper falls slowly because of air resistance. The flat surface of the paper presents a large area for the air to push against. If there were no air resistance—for example, if you conducted your experiment on the moon—then the orange and the sheet of paper would fall at the same rate.

In August 1971 David R. Scott, an astronaut on the Apollo 15 mission, tried such an experiment on the moon. He dropped a hammer and a feather, and they hit at the same time. "How about that," said Scott, "Mr. Galileo was correct!"

Ptolemy's theory of the universe is called a *geocentric* theory. *Ge* is the Greek word for earth. So, geocentric means having the earth as the center. (What other "earth" words can you think of that start with *geo*?)

with the bigger spheres around the smaller spheres, and the earth at the center of all.

For hundreds and hundreds of years, people accepted Ptolemy's description of the universe. No one questioned his views—no one, that is, until a Polish astronomer named Nicolaus Copernicus [koh-PUR-nih-kus] came along.

In the early 1500s, Copernicus was studying the stars. What he saw looked very different from what Ptolemy had written hundreds of years earlier. After Copernicus made careful observations for over twenty years, he came to a startling conclusion: Ptolemy and the ancients are wrong, he said. The earth does not sit still at the center of the universe. Instead, the earth and other planets revolve around the sun!

Copernicus had made a great discovery. But he did not run out and shout it from the rooftops. In fact, he kept very quiet about his news. Why? For one thing, he did not have enough evidence to prove his ideas beyond all doubt. For another, he feared what would happen to him if he publicly contradicted the church's beliefs about the universe. You see, scholars in the church had studied the ideas of Aristotle, Ptolemy, and other ancient philosophers. These church scholars concluded that the ideas of the ancients, which put humans at the center of the universe, supported what the Bible said. So the church assumed the ancient theories were true.

In contrast to Ptolemy's geocentric theory, Copernicus offered a *heliocentric* description of the universe. *Helios* is the Greek work for sun. So heliocentric means having the sun as the center.

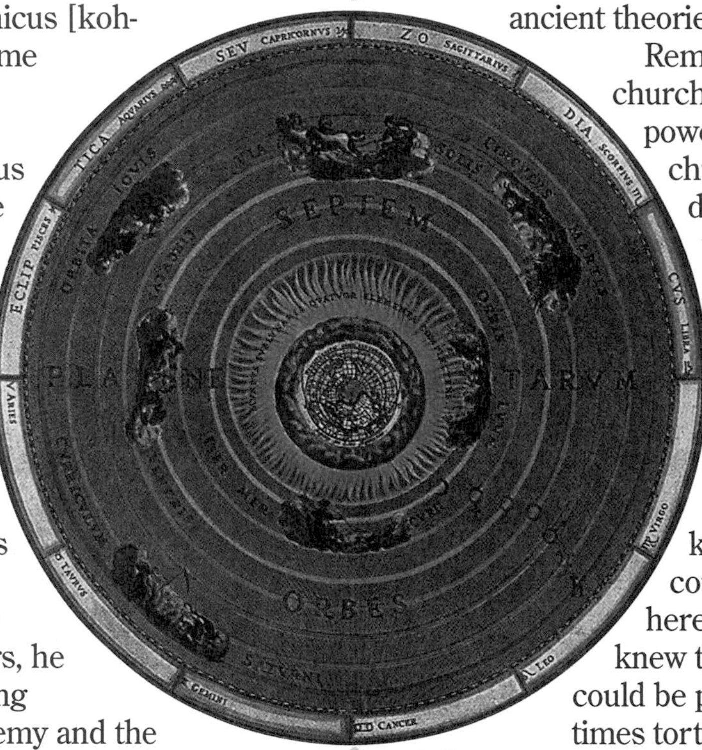

A diagram of Ptolemy's geocentric model of the universe

Remember, the church was very powerful. When church leaders decided something was true, they expected everyone else to believe it, too. That is why Copernicus kept quiet. He knew the church could call him a heretic, and he knew that heretics could be punished, sometimes tortured or even executed.

Not until 1543, at the very end of his life, did Copernicus publish his findings in a book called *On the Revolutions of the Celestial Spheres*. Some people say that Copernicus was handed the first printed copy of his book on the day that he died.

At first, Copernicus's new ideas did not get much attention or cause much disturbance, though Martin Luther did call Copernicus "the fool [who] wants to turn the whole art of astronomy upside down." But then, Galileo came along.

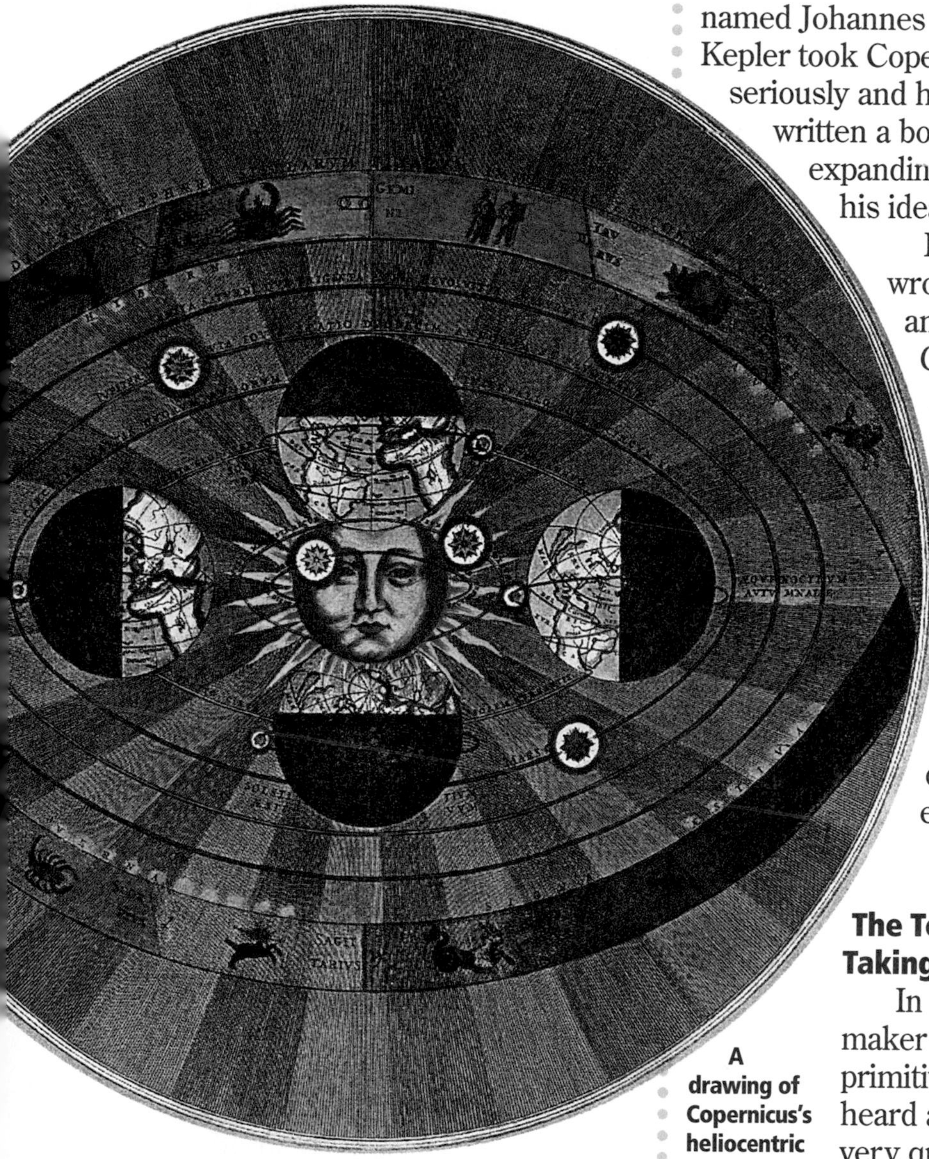

A drawing of Copernicus's heliocentric model of the universe

Galileo Agrees with Copernicus

Galileo's father wanted him to study medicine, so at the age of seventeen Galileo headed off to the University of Pisa. But after only a couple of years, he left medical school to study and then teach mathematics.

During these years, Galileo studied Copernicus's ideas about the universe and became convinced that Copernicus was right. In fact, he wrote a letter saying so to a German astronomer named Johannes Kepler. Kepler took Copernicus seriously and had written a book expanding on his ideas.

Copernicus

Kepler wrote back and urged Galileo to tell others his ideas. But at this point, Galileo, like Copernicus, did not want to fight with the church. He felt he needed more evidence to prove his ideas were right. Over the next several years, Galileo discovered the evidence he needed.

The Telescope: Taking a Closer Look

In 1608, a Dutch glass maker constructed a primitive telescope. Galileo heard about the idea and very quickly improved on the design. He brought his telescope to Venice, where it instantly became popular with soldiers, sailors, and noblemen.

When Galileo looked up at the night sky with his telescope, he saw much that directly contradicted the ideas of Aristotle and Ptolemy. They believed that all heavenly bodies were perfect spheres. But through his telescope Galileo saw that the moon was not

An excited Galileo demonstrates how the telescope works.

perfectly smooth, as people had long believed, but instead had a rough surface marked with mountains, valleys, and craters. Aristotle and Ptolemy also believed the heavens were complete; they thought nothing new could ever appear there. But with his telescope Galileo saw what he thought were some new planets circling Jupiter. (We now know they are really Jupiter's moons.)

Galileo probably thought, "At last, here is the evidence I need. I only have to show my fellow scientists the facts and they will see the truth."

In 1610, Galileo published a book, *The Starry Messenger*, in which he described what he had seen through his telescope. The public loved his book, but Galileo was wrong about the scientists and scholars. Those men seemed to fear change more than they loved truth. They cried out against Galileo, saying he was wrong, even evil. They labeled him a heretic and encouraged priests and monks to condemn him. Soon, important members of the church began to speak against Galileo.

Galileo considered himself both a believer in God and a good Catholic. He didn't think his ideas challenged the church or the Bible. He thought science and religion answered different questions. He said the purpose of the Bible was to show "how one goes to heaven, not how the heavens go."

Galileo wrote letters and gave speeches in order to defend himself and Copernicus's views. But things only got worse, especially when Galileo got into trouble with the Inquisition.

The Inquisition: The Enforcers!

Inquisition—the word can send chills up a person's spine. The Inquisition was another name for the Holy Office, which was the court of the Roman Catholic Church that had the power to accuse and judge people for the crime of heresy—of holding beliefs that went against the church.

Why was the Inquisition so scary? Because, for a time, it was very powerful, and very cruel. People who were found guilty of heresy could be tortured or even executed for their beliefs.

In 1615, the Inquisition discussed Galileo and the ideas of Copernicus for over two months. They decided that the ideas of Copernicus contradicted the Bible. They ordered Galileo to stop thinking or teaching that the earth moves.

Galileo

Galileo had a choice. He could keep discussing his ideas about the universe and risk imprisonment or torture. Or he could stay safe by keeping quiet.

Galileo did keep quiet for a little while. However, when a new pope, Urban VIII, came into power, Galileo hoped that this new man with new ideas would listen to him.

In 1624, Galileo asked Pope Urban for permission to write a book that would discuss the ocean tides in relation to the contrasting ideas of Ptolemy and Copernicus. Surprisingly, the pope gave Galileo permission to write the book.

When it was published in 1632, Galileo's *Dialogue on the Two Chief World Systems* created a great stir. The book was written in Italian, not Latin, so the man on the street could read it. Also, Galileo presented the information in a clear and humorous way, so the man on the street would want to read it. With the aid of the printing press, the book quickly got into in the hands of many people.

This success backfired for Galileo. Think about it. If the book had been written in Latin and stayed behind the walls of universities and monasteries, it would not have presented much of a threat. But because so many people were reading and talking about the book, Galileo's enemies became even more convinced that he had to be stopped.

Scholars and philosophers were angry at Galileo. He had done too good a job of making fun of ancient, mistaken ideas. Now the scholars and philosophers who still clung to these old ideas felt as if people were laughing at them. (And they probably were!)

Church leaders worried that if ordinary people were allowed to question the church's ideas about the universe, they might begin to question other teachings of the church. The church feared losing its power to lead the people.

Not everyone disagreed with Galileo. A few philosophers, scientists, and men of the church supported him and were concerned for his safety. But they were not the ones in power.

Galileo on Trial

From here on, Galileo's is a sad story. In 1632, the Inquisition accused him of heresy and ordered him to come to Rome to stand trial. At the age of seventy, Galileo was weak and sick. He pleaded that he was too ill to make the trip. The pope insisted, so Galileo had to be carried the whole way on a stretcher.

During his trial, Galileo was falsely accused of using trickery to get permission to write the *Dialogue*. The men of the Inquisition insisted that Galileo confess and take back his support for the ideas of Copernicus. Galileo knew that if he did not bend, he faced torture and possibly death by being burned at the stake. So, in 1633, he publicly stated that the sun is not at the center of the universe and that the earth does not move.

According to some accounts, however, as Galileo left the trial he whispered, "But it *does* move!"

Final Justice for Galileo

Flash forward to the year 1979, more than 300 years after the trial of Galileo. What happened in 1979 that could possibly have anything to do with Galileo? A lot. In 1979, Pope John Paul II opened an investigation into the trial and condemnation of Galileo. Three years later, the pope acknowledged that church officials had made a mistake when they condemned the astronomer. At last, Galileo was cleared of wrongdoing.

Galileo Gets the Last Word

The Inquisition punished Galileo by forcing him to live under guard in a house for the rest of his life. He could no longer publish or discuss his ideas, and his books were banned at all the universities.

Banning the *Dialogue* made it a best seller overnight. Even though, or maybe because, it was illegal to own or read the book, everyone wanted a copy. The book was distributed all over Europe and beyond.

Galileo did not spend the last ten years of his life dozing by a crackling fire. He spent the time writing an important book on physics. Several years later, the English scientist Sir Isaac Newton, known as the father of modern physics, used Galileo's ideas as a starting point for his theories. (You may wonder how Galileo managed to write another book without being persecuted. A friend smuggled the manuscript to Holland where it was published under another name.)

Galileo changed the world of science forever. He demanded that we learn about the universe around us by experiment and observation. He insisted that theories be supported by evidence. He had the courage to question accepted authorities and pursue the truth.

Epilogue
Ciao, Bambino!

Congratulations! You made it. You've finished this book and I hope you've learned a lot.

You found out the Renaissance was a time when people rediscovered classical Greek and Roman art and ideas. You learned that many Renaissance artists used the ancient works as an inspiration for their own spectacular achievements in sculpture, painting, and architecture.

You've read about plague-infested rats, an art-loving Italian family, a warrior pope, an extraordinary woman, a brilliant painter who wanted to fly, and many great artists. You've encountered the smooth manners of a courtier and the Machiavellian scheming of a prince. You've met two great writers, one who gave us the story of a "quixotic" knight, and the other who wrote the greatest plays of all time.

Then you found out about the Reformation—and now you know what a papal bull is! You learned about the invention of the printing press and the power of the printed word. You met Martin Luther, whose tough questions led to the division of Christianity into Catholicism and Protestantism. You saw how the Catholic church tried to reform itself, but not always in good ways, such as when it banned books or put Galileo on trial.

The Renaissance and Reformation were amazing, extraordinary times. I hope you'll keep on learning about the people, art, music, literature, and ideas you've been introduced to here.

And now, all I have left to say is, "*Ciao, bambino*!"

Chronology

***c.* = *circa*, which is Latin for "about."**

1304 Birth of Petrarch
1337 Beginning of Hundred Years' War between England and France
***c.* 1347-51** The Plague or Black Death kills millions of people in Europe
1364 Charles V becomes King of France
1374 Death of Petrarch
1377 Birth of Brunelleschi
***c.* 1386** Birth of Donatello
1389 Birth of Cosimo de' Medici
***c.* 1390** Birth of Jan Van Eyck
1403 Ghiberti wins competition for design of second set of Baptistery doors
***c.* 1415** Portugal's Prince Henry "the Navigator" urges exploration of African coast
1415-1417 Donatello carves the statue *St. George*
1420 Work begins on the dome, designed by Brunelleschi, of Florence Cathedral
1434 Cosimo de' Medici begin his thirty-year influence over Florence
***c.* 1440** Birth of the composer Josquin Desprez
1441 Death of Jan Van Eyck
***c.* 1445** Birth of Botticelli
1446 Death of Brunelleschi
1449 Birth of Lorenzo de' Medici
***c.* 1450** Gutenberg starts priniting using movable type
1452 Birth of Leonardo da Vinci
1453 Hundred Years' War between England and France ends
Turks capture Constantinople, marks end of Byzantine Empire; many scholars flee to Italy, bringing Greek writings and other books
1466 Death of Donatello
1469 Lorenzo de' Medici begins rule of Florence
Birth of Machiavelli
Spain's King Ferdinand and Isabella marry
1471 Birth of Dürer
1473 Birth of Copernicus
1475 Birth of Michelangelo
***c.* 1477** Birth of Titian
***c.* 1478** Giuliano de' Medici murdered in Florence Cathedral
1482 Da Vinci goes to work at court of Lodovico Sforza in Milan
1483 Birth of Martin Luther
Birth of Raphael
Richard III becomes King of England
1488 Bartolomeu Dias rounds the Cape of Good Hope
1492 Alexander VI (Rodrigo Borgia) becomes Pope
Columbus sails across the Atlantic to the "New World"
Spain conquers Granada, expels Islamic Moors from Iberian Peninsula
Lorenzo de' Medici dies
Da Vinci draws a flying machine in his notebook
1493 Pope Alexander VI issues a papal bull dividing the "New World" between Spain and Portugal
1494 King Charles VIII of France invades Italy
Medicis leave Florence
Dürer visits Italy for first time
1494-1497 Savonarola controls Florence
***c.* 1495-1497** Da Vinci paints *The Last Supper*
1497 John Cabot sails from England to coast of Newfoundland
1497-98 Vasco da Gama sails to India
1498 Savonarola burned at stake for heresy
1500 Cabral claims Brazil for Portugal
1501 Michangelo begins *David*
1502 Da Vinci becomes Cesare Borgia's military engineer and chief architect
1503 Pope Alexander VI dies, his son Cesare Borgia loses power
1503 Julius II (art patron) becomes pope
1504 Michangelo completes *David*
1506 Da Vinci completes *Mona Lisa*
Pope Julius II orders work on St. Peter's Basilica
1508 Michelangelo begins work on the Sistine Chapel ceiling

1509 Raphael begins work on the Vatican rooms
Henry VIII becomes King of England and marries Catherine of Aragon
Birth of John Calvin
1510 Death of Botticelli
1512 Michelangelo finishes the ceiling of the Sistine Chapel
Medicis back in power in Florence
1513 Balboa reaches the Pacific Ocean
Ponce de Leon lands in Florida
Pope Julius II dies, succeeded by Leo X (Giovanni, son of Lorenzo de' Medici)
Machiavelli writes *The Prince*
1515 King Francis I of France invades Italy, brings Italian artists to work at his court
1517 Martin Luther posts his Ninety-five Theses, the Reformation begins
1519 Death of Leonardo da Vinci
Charles V (King of Spain) becomes the Holy Roman Emperor
1520 Raphael dies
1521 Martin Luther declared a heretic by the Diet of Worms
Death of Josquin Desprez
Cortes conquers the Aztecs of Mexico, destroys Tenochtitlán
1522 Martin Luther comes out of hiding and goes back to Wittenberg
Magellan's expedition returns to Spain after circling the world
***c.* 1525** Birth of the composer Palestrina
Birth of Pieter Bruegel the Elder
1527 Death of Machiavelli
1528 Castiglione's *The Courtier* published
Death of Dürer
1530 Copernicus completes (but does not publish) *On the Revolutions of the Celestial Spheres*, asserting that the earth revolves around the sun
1533 Pizarro conquers the Inca of Peru
1534 Martin Luther finishes his translation of the New Testament of the Bible into German
Henry VIII becomes supreme head of Church of England, breaks with Rome
1536-41 Michelangelo paints *The Last Judgment* in the Sistine Chapel
1538 Calvin expelled from Geneva
1541 Calvin returns to Geneva
Hernando de Soto crosses the Mississippi
Coronado explores the American southwest
1543 In the year of his death, Copernicus's *On the Revolutions of the Celestial Spheres* is published
1545 Council of Trent, beginning of the Counter Reformation
1546 Death of Martin Luther
1547 Death of King Henry VIII of England
Birth of Cervantes
1550 Vasari's *Lives of the Artists* published
1556 Philip II becomes King of Spain and ruler of Sicily, Milan, and Naples
1558 Elizabeth I becomes Queen of England
1562 Birth of the composer John Dowland
1564 Death of Michelangelo
Birth of Shakespeare
1571 Cervantes injured in the naval Battle of Lepanto
1576 Death of Titian
1594 Death of Palestrina
***c.* 1595** Shakespeare writes *Romeo and Juliet*
1605 Part I of Cervantes's *Don Quixote* published
1608 Champlain founds a French settlement at Québec
1609 Henry Hudson explores the Hudson River
1615 Part II of Cervantes's *Don Quixote* published
1616 Death of Shakespeare
Death of Cervantes
1626 Death of Dowland
1632 Galileo's *Dialogue on the Two Chief World Systems* published
1633 Galileo is forced by the Inquisition to deny his discoveries
1642 Death of Galileo
Birth of Isaac Newton

Afterword
On History for Young Readers

by E. D. Hirsch, Jr.

The non-profit Core Knowledge Foundation is publishing this and other books in the Core Chronicles series in response to requests from teachers and parents for good children's books that narrate the fascinating sweep of world history outlined in the Core Knowledge Sequence.[1] We hope that these books, like the exemplary works of Jean Fritz or Joy Hakim's *History of US* series, will vividly convey a sense of the past and its implicit lessons about human nature through the ages, as well as give children a context for understanding the more detailed history they will study later.

In recent years, our schools have taught very little history in the elementary grades, except for local and state history in fourth grade, followed by a cursory survey of U. S. history in fifth. In contrast, the history guidelines of the Core Knowledge Sequence have surprised and delighted many teachers and parents by returning to the earlier American tradition of presenting substantial history in early grades on a range of topics from ancient Egypt in first grade to current events in eighth. Thomas Jefferson argued forcefully that history should be the chief topic of early education in a democracy. It's true that later Ralph Waldo Emerson mocked history and Henry Ford said it was "bunk," but there are good reasons to believe that Jefferson's is the sounder view.

In 1987, Diane Ravitch, the eminent historian of education, published an important article called "Tot Sociology, or What Happened to History in the Grade Schools." She called attention to "the curious nature of the early grades, which is virtually content-free" because it is dominated by the curriculum model of "expanding horizons"—a series of concentric circles at the center of which is "The Child." According to the expanding horizons model, schools should begin by teaching the child about herself and only gradually move into larger circles, from The Child outward to The Family, The School, The Community, and so on. Originating in the 1930s and based on hunches rather than sound science, expanding horizons effectively banished history from the primary grades and replaced it with a curriculum of "me, my family, my school, my community."[2]

While it is true that the process of learning moves from the familiar to the unfamiliar, the educators who invented the expanding horizons model failed to take account of how "familiar" and exciting to children are things they have never seen, like elves or fairies. The theorists of the '30s, assuming that the child's real interest is in the immediate and the personal, omitted to explain why children are in fact so interested in dinosaurs, medieval castles, and knights in armor.

In the course of the next decades, early-childhood educators came to assume that expanding horizons represented the accumulated wisdom of generations of educational research. As Ravitch explained: "Teachers believe that ...[it] is there because it has always been there." In fact, the model has existed for only five or six decades and it displaced a longstanding American tradition of teaching history to very young children. Ravitch found, for example, that early in the twentieth century the curriculum for *third grade* in the Philadelphia public schools required the study of "heroes of legend and history," including "Joseph; Moses; David; Ulysses; Alexander; Horatius; Cincinnatus; Siegfried; Arthur; Roland; Alfred the Great; Richard the Lion Hearted; Robert Bruce; William Tell; Joan of Arc; Peter the Great; [and] Florence Nightingale." The curriculum was designed "to introduce children to exciting stories of important events and significant individuals and to provide them with a basic historical and cultural vocabulary"—which is a good description of the purposes of the history outlined in the Core Knowledge Sequence.

Although the ideas of the 1930s no longer apply today, many educators perpetuate the old anti-content prejudice in more up-to-date language. Instead of arguing, as in the 1930s, that expanding horizons "would better prepare children for real life through its emphasis on everyday life, social-mindedness, realistic problems, and problem solving," educators today are likely to claim that the early study of history is "developmentally inappropriate," or wastes time on the "rote learning" of "mere facts." The words have changed, but the music is the same. The underlying, anti-historical, even anti-intellectual sentiments are made no sounder through continued repetition than they were when first pulled out of a pseudo-scientific hat half a century ago.

The aim of these books in the Core Chronicles series is introductory. They attempt to avoid the arid summaries that make students dislike history because "it's just a bunch of names and dates." They emphasize the story in history. They include some familiar legends (acknowledging them as such), because even inaccurate traditional legends such as the story of George Washington and the cherry tree sometimes convey an important historical lesson or an essential quality of a person. They attempt to avoid the common sin of textbooks—covering everything and exploring nothing—by taking a more selective focus. While selectivity always leaves the historian open to criticism for the sin of omission, that is a lesser sin than dullness, especially in early books designed to sharpen the curiosity of children and inspire them to learn more about the world beyond their immediate surroundings—the most fruitful way to expand their horizons.

NOTES

[1] For information about the Core Knowledge Sequence, see page 101, "About Core Knowledge."

[2] Diane Ravitch, "Tot Sociology, or What Happened to History in the Grade Schools," *American Scholar* 56 (Summer 1987). Since Ravitch's article, and to some extent in response to it, there have been positive developments, such as the creation of voluntary National Standards in History, though these have been marred by controversy. A promising portent is the inclusion of specific historical content standards in early grades in the revised Virginia Standards of Learning (1995) and in the Massachusetts History and Social Science Curriculum Framework (1997).

Resources

Art and Artists

Albrecht Dürer by Ernest Raboff (HarperCollins, 1988)

The Art of the Renaissance by Lucia Corrain (Peter Bedrick Books, 1997)

Leonardo da Vinci by Antony Mason (Barron's, 1994)

Leonardo da Vinci by Richard McLanathan (Harry N. Abrams, 1990)

Leonardo Da Vinci: Artist, Inventor and Scientist of the Renaissance by Francesca Romei (Peter Bedrick Books, 1994)

Michelangelo by Jen Green (Barron's, 1993)

Michelangelo by Richard McLanathan (Harry N. Abrams, 1993)

Michelangelo and His Times by Véronique Milande (Henry Holt, 1996)

Michelangelo Buonarroti (1988) by Ernest Raboff (HarperCollins, 1988)

The Story of Art by E.H. Gombrich (1950; 16th ed., Phaidon Press, 1995)

What Makes a Bruegel a Bruegel? by Richard Mühlberger (Viking/ Metropolitan Museum of Art, 1993)

What Makes a Leonardo a Leonardo? by Richard Mühlberger (Viking/ Metropolitan Museum of Art, 1994)

What Makes a Raphael a Raphael? by Richard Mühlberger (Viking/ Metropolitan Museum of Art, 1993)

Related History

Around the World in a Hundred Years: From Henry the Navigator to Magellan by Jean Fritz (G. P. Putnam's Sons, 1994)

Breaking into Print: Before and After the Invention of the Printing Press by Stephen Krensky (Little, Brown and Co., 1996)

Gutenberg by Leonard Everett Fisher (Macmillan, 1993)

"Islamic Spain," *Calliope* magazine (Nov./Dec. 1995, Vol. 6 No. 2)

"Monasteries in Medieval Europe," *Calliope* magazine (January 1998, Vol. 8 No. 5)

The Renaissance ("See Through History" series) by Tim Wood (Viking, 1993)

Music (Compact Disc Recordings)

JOSQUIN DESPREZ

Missa L'homme armé, Oxford Camerata (Naxos 8.553428)

Motets and Chansons, The Hilliard Ensemble (Virgin Veritas 61302)

Renaissance: The Music of Josquin Desprez, The King's Singers (RCA 61814)

PALESTRINA

Missa Papae Marcelli, Oxford Camerata (Naxos 8.550573)

JOHN DOWLAND

Consort Music and Lute Songs, Rose Consort of Viols (Naxos 8.553326)

Complete Lute Works Vol. 4 (with "Lachrimae"), Paul O'Dette (Harmonia Mundi 907163)

COLLECTIONS

An Introduction to Early Music (Naxos 8.551203)

1492: Music from the Age of Discovery, The Waverly Consort (EMI 54506)

Greensleeves: A Collection of English Lute Songs, Julianne Baird and Ronn McFarlane (Dorian 90126)

Literature

Bard of Avon: The Story of William Shakespeare by Diane Stanley and Peter Vennema (William Morrow, 1992)

Don Quixote (Core Classics series) by Miguel de Cervantes, ed. Michael Marshall (Core Knowledge Foundation, 1999)

A Midsummer Night's Dream for Young People and *Romeo and Juliet for Young People* edited by Diane Davidson (Swan Books, 1986)

The Second Mrs. Giaconda by E. L. Konigsburg (Aladdin Books, 1975)

The World of Shakespeare by Anna Claybourne and Rebecca Treays (Usborne, 1997)

About Core Knowledge

Core Knowledge is a curricular reform model that emphasizes teaching a common core of knowledge in the early grades.

This core is defined in the Core Knowledge Sequence, a planned progression of specific topics in history, geography, mathematics, science, language arts, visual arts, and music. The hallmark of the Sequence is its specificity. From preschool through eighth grade, the Sequence maps out a clear progression of knowledge that builds grade by grade, including, for example, Ancient Egypt, Greece and Rome, and African kingdoms; the solar system, electric circuits, and photosynthesis; American tall tales, Shakespeare, and the Harlem Renaissance.

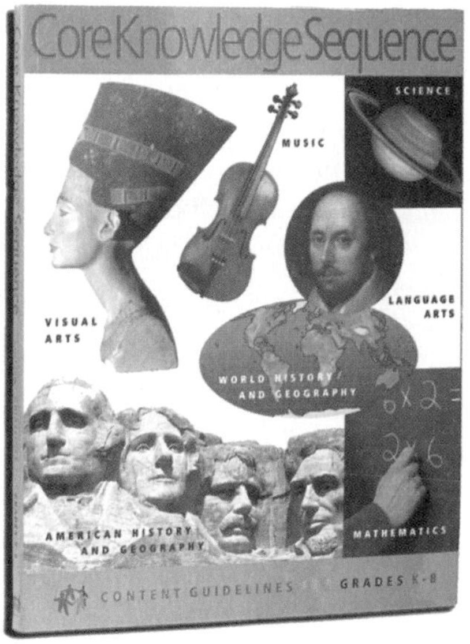

The Core Knowledge Sequence: Content Guidelines for Grades K-8

The Core Knowledge Sequence is the result of research into the successful educational systems of several other countries, as well as a long process of consensus-building including parents, teachers, scientists, and experts on America's multicultural traditions.

Founded in 1986 by E. D. Hirsch, Jr., a professor at the University of Virginia and author of *Cultural Literacy: What Every American Needs to Know* (1987) and *The Schools We Need and Why We Don't Have Them* (1994), the non-profit Core Knowledge Foundation conducts research on educational issues and ideas, develops books and other materials to support the teaching of the Sequence, and provides training for schools seeking to implement Core Knowledge programs.

***Don Quixote,* from the Core Classics series**

For more information and for a free catalogue of Core Knowledge books and other resources, please write or call

Core Knowledge Foundation
801 East High Street
Charlottesville, VA 22902

TELEPHONE: (804) 977-7550
FAX: (804) 977-0021
E-MAIL: coreknow@coreknowledge.org
HOME PAGE: www.coreknowledge.org

Earnings from sales of Core Knowledge publications go to the non-profit Core Knowledge Foundation.
E. D. Hirsch, Jr. receives no remuneration from the Core Knowledge Foundation.

Index

Illustration and Photo Credits

While every care has been taken to trace and acknowledge copyright, the editors tender their apologies for any accidental infringement where copyright has proved untraceable. They would be pleased to insert the appropriate acknowledgment in any subsequent edition of this publication.

Art Resource, NY: 59(a)
Erich Lessing/Art Resource, NY: 24(b), 30, 33, 39(a), 42(c), 55(b), 58(b), 61
Giraudon/Art Resource, NY: 12, 59(c)
Scala/Art Resource, NY: 7(b), 10, 13, 15(a), 18(a), 25, 28-29, 34, 42(b), 49, 50(a), 51, 52(a), 53, 55(c), 60(b), 63
© Copyright the British Museum, London.: 32(a)
CALVIN AND HOBBES © 1993 Watterson. Reprinted with permission of UNIVERSAL PRESS SYNDICATE. All rights reserved.: 7(a)
Corbis/Bettmann: Cover, 2, 9(a), 38, 74 , 77, 90-91, 93
Corbis/Archivo Iconografico, S.A.: 6(a), 23, 31 87, 89
Corbis/Arte & Immagini srl: 42(a), 46, 47(a), 54(a)
Corbis/James L. Amos: 40-41
Corbis/Hulton-Deutsch Collection: 85
Corbis/Kit Kittle: 52(b)
Corbis/David Lees: 19(a), 20, 80
Corbis/Araldo de Luca: 45
Corbis/Francis G. Mayer: 43(a), 58(a)
Corbis/Gianni Dagli Orti : 35(b). 37(a), 59(b), 76
Tricia Emlet: 41
The Globe Theatre (reconstruction) at the International Shakespeare Globe Centre, London. Pentagram Design Ltd., architects. Photo © F.J. Hildy: 73(a)
Steve Henry: 1, 17, 24(a), 26(a), 32(c), 43(b), 50(b), 64(b), 72, 78(b), 83, 88(b), 95
Bob Kirchman: 47(b)
Knight, Death, and the Devil, 1513, by Albrecht Dürer; German (Nuremburgh, 1471-1528); Engraving; 243 x 189 mm; Museum of Fine Arts, Boston; Bequest of Mrs. Horatio G. Curtis: 60(a)
Library of Congress: 56, 66-67, 70, 82
Lorenzo de' Medici, probably after a model by A. Verrocchio and O. Benintendi, Samuel H. Kress Collection, © 1998 Board of Trustees, National Gallery of Art Washington, DC: 16(a)
North Winds Pictures: 19(b)
Raphael, The Small Cowper Madonna, Widener Collection, © 1998 Board of Trustees, National Gallery of Art, Washington, D.C.:19(b)
School of Athens, 1510-11 (fresco) by Raphael (Raffaello Sanzio of Urbino) (1483-1520), Vatican Museums and Galleries, Vatican City, Italy/Bridgeman Art Library: 55(a)
Still from "WILLIAM SHAKESPEARE'S ROMEO AND JULIET" © 1997 Twentieth Century Fox Corporation. All rights reserved. Photograph courtesy of the Academy of Motion Picture Arts and Sciences: 71
Stock Montage: 15(b), 16(b), 21, 52(c), 70-71, 86, 90, 91, 92

About the Author

DEBORAH MAZZOTTA PRUM and her husband are raising three sons in Charlottesville, Virginia. She has written short stories for adults and children, as well as magazine articles for adults and teens. She drew and sold cartoons to help pay her way through college and graduate school (the University of Connecticut and Dartmouth College). Like Leonardo da Vinci, she plays string music. Leonardo played the lute; Debby plays banjo and mandolin.